THE WONDER
YOU

A self discovery journal

Dr Maxine Thérèse

child◯sophy

Copyright © by Maxine Thérèse 2019 Childosophy™

Artwork hand drawn by Melanie Bedford & altered by Jodie Beckley
Artwork is copyrighted by Childosophy™

Journal design by thesqueezebox.com.au

All rights reserved. No part of this journal may be reproduced by any mechanical, photographic, or electronic process, or in the form of phonographic recording; nor may it be stored on a retrieval system, transmitted, or otherwise be copied for public or private use – other than for 'fair use' as brief quotations embodied in articles and reviews without prior written permission of the author. The intent of the author is to offer information of a general nature to children's wellbeing and makes no claims otherwise.

www.childosophy.com

This journal is dedicated to children who have been waiting for a map that helps them understand their feelings, thoughts and actions.

THIS JOURNAL BELONGS TO:

In this Journal

A note for parents 11
The Wonder of You 15
The Wonder of Your Needs 18
Your Foundational Needs 20
The BODY map of your needs 23
BE in the Wonder of YOU 24
Staying Open to the Wonder of YOU! 26

I AM SAFE .... 29 ☐
I am Safe and Secure .... 30 ☐
I feel Safe and Secure when .... 34 ☐
Safe and Secure feelings .... 36 ☐
Unsafe and Insecure feelings .... 37 ☐
Listen to your body's wisdom .... 38 ☐
Body Mapping Your Feelings – Feet .... 40 ☐
A Moment to Wonder .... 44 ☐
Breathe Safe and Secure – A Meditation .... 46 ☐
I Can Affirm Myself .... 48 ☐
My Tribe .... 50 ☐
Interview – Map your family's Safety and Security 52 ☐
Nature's Abundance .... 54 ☐
Word Search .... 58 ☐
My Safe and Secure Touchstone .... 61 ☐

I AM FREE

I am emotionally free .... 64 ☐
I feel Freedom when .... 66 ☐
Free Flowing Feelings .... 68 ☐
Harder to Move feelings .... 69 ☐
Listen to your body's wisdom .... 70 ☐
Body Mapping Your Feelings - Hip Area .... 72 ☐
A Moment to Wonder .... 76 ☐
Breathe through big emotions - A Meditation .... 78 ☐
I am happiest when .... 80 ☐
I have been ignoring these feelings .... 82 ☐
Lets get cooking .... 86 ☐
Interview - Map your family's feelings .... 88 ☐
Word Search .... 90 ☐
My Emotional Freedom Touchstone .... 93 ☐

I ACT .... 95 ☐

I act .... 96 ☐
I feel in alignment when .... 98 ☐
Strengthening feelings .... 100 ☐
Weakening feelings .... 101 ☐
Listen to your body's wisdom .... 102 ☐
Body Mapping Your Feelings - Stomach .... 104 ☐
A Moment to Wonder .... 108 ☐
Breathe through indecision - A Meditation .... 110 ☐
I can do these things .... 112 ☐

When I'm aligned with my Soul .... 114 ☐
When I have trouble doing something .... 115 ☐
Interview – Map your family's Team Work .... 116 ☐
Word Search .... 118 ☐
My Achievement Touchstone .... 121 ☐

I AM LOVE .... 123 ☐
I am love and I am loved .... 124 ☐
I feel loved and loving when .... 126 ☐
Loving feelings .... 128 ☐
Unloving feelings .... 129 ☐
Listen to your body's wisdom .... 130 ☐
Body Mapping Your Feelings – Heart .... 132 ☐
A Moment to Wonder .... 136 ☐
Breathe through Anger – A Meditation .... 138 ☐
What a pet might need to be loved .... 140 ☐
These things I love about others and me .... 142 ☐
Gratitude Beads .... 144 ☐
Interview – Map your family's Love .... 146 ☐
Word Search .... 148 ☐
My Love Touchstone .... 151 ☐

I SPEAK .... 153 ☐
I speak .... 154 ☐
I can speak and I am heard when .... 158 ☐
High vibration speech .... 160 ☐

Low vibration speech .... 161 ☐
Listen to your body's wisdom .... 162 ☐
Body Mapping Your Feelings – Teeth .... 164 ☐
A Moment to Wonder .... 168 ☐
Breathe – I express – A Meditation .... 170 ☐
Charades .... 172 ☐
How would you communicate .... 174 ☐
Interview – Map your family's speech .... 176 ☐
Word Search .... 178 ☐
My being heard Touchstone .... 181 ☐

I IMAGINE .... 183 ☐
I See .... 184 ☐
I see my way out of a learning challenger when ...... 188 ☐
Expansive feelings .... 190 ☐
Contracting feelings .... 191 ☐
Listen to your body's wisdom .... 192 ☐
Body mapping Your Feelings – Brain .... 194 ☐
A Moment to Wonder .... 198 ☐
Breathe – An intention – A Meditation .... 200 ☐
Mind Mapping .... 202 ☐
Interview – Map your family's worries .... 204 ☐
Wonder Jar .... 206 ☐
Word Search .... 208 ☐
My Clarity Touchstone .... 211 ☐

I KNOW	213 ☐
I am all know-ing	214 ☐
I feel connected to the universe when	218 ☐
Unifying feelings	220 ☐
Separating feelings	221 ☐
Listen to your body's wisdom	222 ☐
Body mapping Your Feelings – Skin	224 ☐
A Moment to Wonder	228 ☐
Breathe – Self awareness – A Meditation	230 ☐
Interview – Map your family's Meaning	232 ☐
Crystal Grid	234 ☐
Word Search	236 ☐
My connected and whole Touchstone	239 ☐

Look at the Wonder of You	241
Listen to your body's wisdom	243
A Moment To Wonder	245
Map Your family's WONDER	246
My Touchstones Table	248
Acknowledgements	251
About the Author	252

A note for parents

The Wonder Of You Journal by Childosophy has been designed with the intention of lovingly supporting children to know themselves from the very beginnings so they experience life in the wonder of who they truly are.

The journal is aimed to prompt wonder in your child. To wonder about why they feel certain things, and what their feelings, thoughts and emotions mean to them. And that when they experience certain behaviours that seem uneasy or problematic, for them they can be in the wonder about what Foundational Need this all correlates with. The Foundational Needs in this journal are based on my research that mapped children's behaviours and actions to foundational needs. I found that all behaviours have a special meaning for children about their best growth and that children need to know this meaning for themselves if they are to experience wellbeing and know the Wonder of who they are.

By using the journal, your children will begin to identify and heal their own specific unmet needs and also learn a language of need to be able to communicate their feelings and thoughts with you in a way not possible before. Through the practice of using the journal, your child is unconsciously and symbiotically absorbing that there is nothing 'wrong' when they experience certain feelings or act in certain ways. It helps them to trust that their needs matter, and supports them to understand what their body is communicating through their behaviours.

The journal also empowers children with self-knowledge, to act in a way that is aligned with their best growth. This level of self-awareness allows children to remain centered, balanced and connected to their wholeness regardless of the many influences they encounter from external situations or people. They begin to flow more freely in their day-to-day interactions with themselves, their family and the world.

As parents we can sometimes see our child's behaviours as challenging, disrespectful or worrying. What this journal will help you to know is that even when children's behaviours and responses challenge you — that these responses are always appropriate for the child because they indicate where they have closed the vital flow of energy between what they feel and think. Your children store and hold memory, beliefs and emotions that express in their body and behaviours. Some of these memories, beliefs and emotions are carried over from your own childhood experiences and the experiences of your family line.

This journal gives you an advantage in your parenting as it provides a common language about the needs we all share. As a result of this awareness you will come to see that if your parent's couldn't meet some of your needs, it is most probably because they had difficulty doing this for themselves and they did the best they could with the knowledge available to them. What a gift that we can now communicate with our own children from this evolved space and support their best growth.

Enjoy getting to know the needs of your children as they explore the wonder of who they are.

As you learn from your children what their body is telling them, you will begin to grow together because you will also be reminded of your own body's wisdom and the language of need that your life is communicating. As you remain open and in the wonder with your children, you set the foundation for your healing too and you are ready to support your child's best growth as well as your own at the same time. In fact you might love the process in this journal so much that you want one just for yourself!

In joy, love and wonder,
Dr. Maxine Thérèse.

The Wonder of You

I wonder if you know how amazing you are?

I wonder if you know that your needs matter?

I wonder if you know what these needs are and that they can change, just like the seasons?

Welcome to the Wonder of You Journal.

I am so happy that you are here, about to start your own journey of self-discovery. This journal will help you understand your relationship to yourself as well as all the people, places and events in your life. Once you see how connected we all are, you will see things in a whole new way.

As you work through the pages of the Journal you will become super-clever about your needs. You will learn how what you feel, how you think, and what you believe ALL impact YOU.

You will learn how to listen more closely to the messages of your body. You will come to see how certain things make you feel and what this may mean to you. You will become self-aware and be able to know what you need in any situation.

The beautiful thing about the Wonder of You Journal is that you don't have to complete it in order — it has been designed so that you can read through a need and do the activities that you want based on how you are feeling on any particular day.

You will find words to explain each theme, activities for you to complete — some you can do on your own and some with your family. And you can choose to do all of them or save some for another day, and when you have done them tick them off on the Needs activity checklist starting on page 5. Feel free to write on, draw in, and explore the Wonder of You Journal. It is your own beautiful adventure of self-discovery, which will be different for everyone. There are no right or wrong answers.

We hope you love the Wonder of You Journal as much as we do — we think it's a little bit magical.

The Wonder of Your Needs

Do you know that everyone has needs, even grown-ups, and sometimes when these needs are not met, your body and your life show you this.

You know those days when you are feeling a bit scared or nervous about going to school?

This could mean that you are not feeling safe and secure – the first of the Needs. (The red need – I am safe).

Sometimes this nervousness might give you a shaky body or make you feel weak and this is important information about your need to be safe and secure.

Your Foundational Needs

I AM SAFE

The first need is the Need to Feel Safe and Secure.

This need is all about your connection to the earth and your family as well as your body and its care. If you experience feeling anxious, scared of change, insecure and shaky you can WONDER what you might NEED to feel connected, secure, safe and grounded.

I AM FREE

The second need is The Need to Feel.

This need is all about your emotional freedom and movement. If you experience lack of emotional control, feeling fussy, impulsivity, bedwetting or you get over-excited you can WONDER what you might NEED to feel comfortable with your emotions and be able to flow through uncomfortable emotions with ease.

I ACT

The third need is The Need to Act.

This need is all about your power and your individuality. If you experience stomach aches, bowel pain, defiance, lack of motivation or low self-esteem you can WONDER what you might NEED to feel strong and powerful in your actions and yourself.

I AM LOVE

The fourth need is The Need to Love.

This need is all about your relationships — to yourself, your parents, your siblings, the world and how it all fits together. If you experience breathing issues, asthma, bullying, crying, feel unloved and sad you can WONDER what you might NEED to feel connected, loved and appreciated.

I SPEAK

The fifth need is The Need to Speak.

This need is all about expressing yourself. If you experience speech issues, gagging, feeling unnoticed or uncertain of expressing yourself you can WONDER what you might NEED to feel strong in your words, communicate clearly, and feel listened to.

I IMAGINE

The sixth need is The Need to See.

This need is all about how 'seen' you feel and how well you can visualise things for yourself. If you experience learning challenges, are distracted, feel shy or nervous, or have sleep issues or nightmares you can WONDER what you might NEED to feel seen and noticed, and clear with your vision and intentions.

I KNOW

The seventh need is The Need to Know.

This need is all about the deeper purpose to your life. If you experience growing pains, headaches, skin issues, fainting and dizziness you can WONDER what you might NEED so you can feel confident in your self-knowledge and connected to your highest power and faith.

The BODY Map of Your Needs

Each of your 7 needs has a special spot in your body and is connected to a body part and a body organ. Each need also connects to your emotions — your thought patterns (mindset) and how these affect the way you behave.

Your behaviours and challenges give clues about what may be going on for you — your feelings and thoughts about yourself and the world — and this journal can help you discover what these mean.

None of your feelings, thoughts or behaviours are 'wrong' but they may be hard to understand. You will get to know your feelings, thoughts and behaviours and why they've needed to come out.

And most importantly, you will learn what you can do about them so you can continue feeling balanced and WONDER full.

BE in the Wonder of YOU

Do you know that your body stores and holds the energy of everything you have ever experienced, and these are called memories?

These memories live within the cells of your physical body and shape how your body behaves. If you are naturally good at something or not it is due to the memories that are stored in your body.

The amazing thing is that these memories may not all be your own. Some of these memories may actually belong to your parents or your grandparents. That is why it may be so confusing for you sometimes to understand what you are feeling.

The great news is that these energies can be transformed by being in the question of your feelings and beginning to WONDER about where those feelings come from.

When you know that all of these energy patterns and feelings can be traced back to one of your 7 needs, you have an energetic map to guide you to be the best you can be and create memories that are good for your body and life.

The 7 needs of children are connected to the Chakras.

Have you heard about the Chakras?

Chakras are the main energy points in your body — they are like crossroads or intersections where energy flows back and forth. When one of these centres is blocked — your body will tell you — your feelings, behaviours, emotions and even illness will be telling you that you are imbalanced!

What an amazing map to understand the Wonder of You.

breathe

Staying Open to the Wonder of YOU!

Have you heard the saying 'Listen to your gut' or 'Listen to your heart'? This is just another way of saying to listen to your body's wisdom.

This type of listening is staying open to the WONDER OF YOU!

This listening is not like 'hearing with your ears' or 'thinking' with your brain, but listening by SENSING with your whole body.

You know that feeling in your body when something just doesn't feel right?

When your body closes, feels stuck or uneasy you feel this in your whole body.

That is your body telling you that you have an unmet need — and it's time for you to learn how to work out what it is!

Your body works without you even having to think about it. You don't have to think about breathing – you just do this automatically. When you need to go to the toilet your body 'tells' you to find a toilet! When you have eaten something that is not good for you, your body vomits. (Gross!) But it is actually amazing because your body knows exactly what to do to make itself feel better and balanced.

When we are busy with growing up, we often don't stop long enough to WONDER about our feelings. We may just say 'Oh, I have a tummy ache today.' But we don't really think about WHY we may feel this way. This causes the energy in our bodies to get stuck, so we need to stay open and curious and be in WONDER!

Your body communicates with you all the time and by learning this special, amazing language, you can understand what your body is saying.

By working through the journal, you will begin to see that the feelings you experience are actually your body's way of communicating to you. You can FEEL into each part of the body in each section and FEEL how each Need feels for YOU.

"Yes, I was feeling FUNNY IN MY TUMMY about going to school yesterday, I WONDER what that means?"

I am Safe and Secure

The first of your Foundational Needs is your 'Need to Feel Safe and Secure'.

Every child needs to feel connected to the earth and their own body, to nature and to their family.

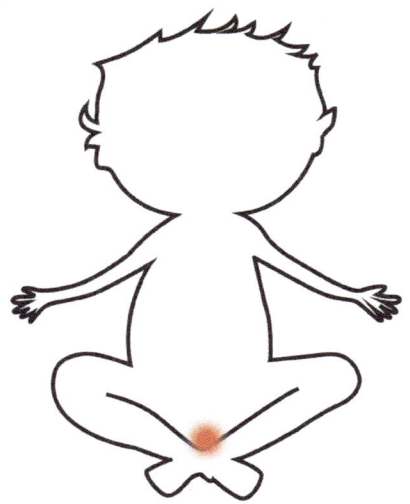

You know that you MUST have these to survive;
- food,
- air,
- water and
- shelter

But in order for you to thrive you also need to feel your safety and security needs are met such as stability, protection, boundaries, nourishment, connection with family and nature, trust, grounding and certainty in self.

Imagine for yourself how secure and safe you are

Can you...

- cope with change?
- stand up for yourself?
- trust your body?
- trust other people?
- know what to do when you are worried?
- have healthy personal boundaries?
- know your routines and daily rituals?

If some of these things are missing or they go unnoticed for too long — think about how that may make you feel?

Uncertain, scared, miserable, unsafe?

These are not always easy to feel.

But when you know that these feelings have important information about what you need, you are more prepared and ready when hard feelings arise.

I feel healthy, nourished and blessed when...

Trusting that the earth and your body will support what you need helps you to feel safe and secure.

I feel safe and secure when...

I can see the door or know the way out.

I am in bed, safe and warm.

When I know how things are supposed to happen.

When I have my special toy or blanket.

When I have a routine and I know what is coming next.

When I can breathe easily.

When I am outside in nature in bare feet.

When my belly is full and I'm not hungry.

When I am in the bath.

When I can see nature or I am close to trees.

When I am in a tent/fort or cubby hole etc.

When both my parents are with me.

When my family is all together.

Circle the ones that feel most true to you, you may find that you have a few.

write the things that make you feel safe and secure in and around the image

Safe and Secure feelings

safe comfortable relaxed
ready grounded
secure
protected calm
certain trusting
boundaries nourished
routines healthy strong

I feel safe in my body when… ……………………………………………
………………………………………………………………………………

I feel calm in my body when… ……………………………………………
………………………………………………………………………………

I feel protected in my body when… ………………………………………
………………………………………………………………………………

Unsafe and insecure feelings

bold uncertain unsafe

rigid jumpy risky doubtful

insecure unsettled defensive

fearful frozen erratic

flighty over-protective

I feel unsafe in my body when... ....

....

I feel scared in my body when... ....

....

I feel unsure in my body when... ....

....

Listen to your body's wisdom

There will be times when you don't feel safe and secure and when this happens it is most important to trust your body and listen to what it is telling you.

Remember this type of listening is not like 'hearing with your ears' or 'thinking' with your brain — but by SENSING with your whole body.

Your need to feel safe and secure is linked to the body locations of your skeleton, your legs, your feet, rectum and your immune system.

See these highlighted on the next page.

skeleton

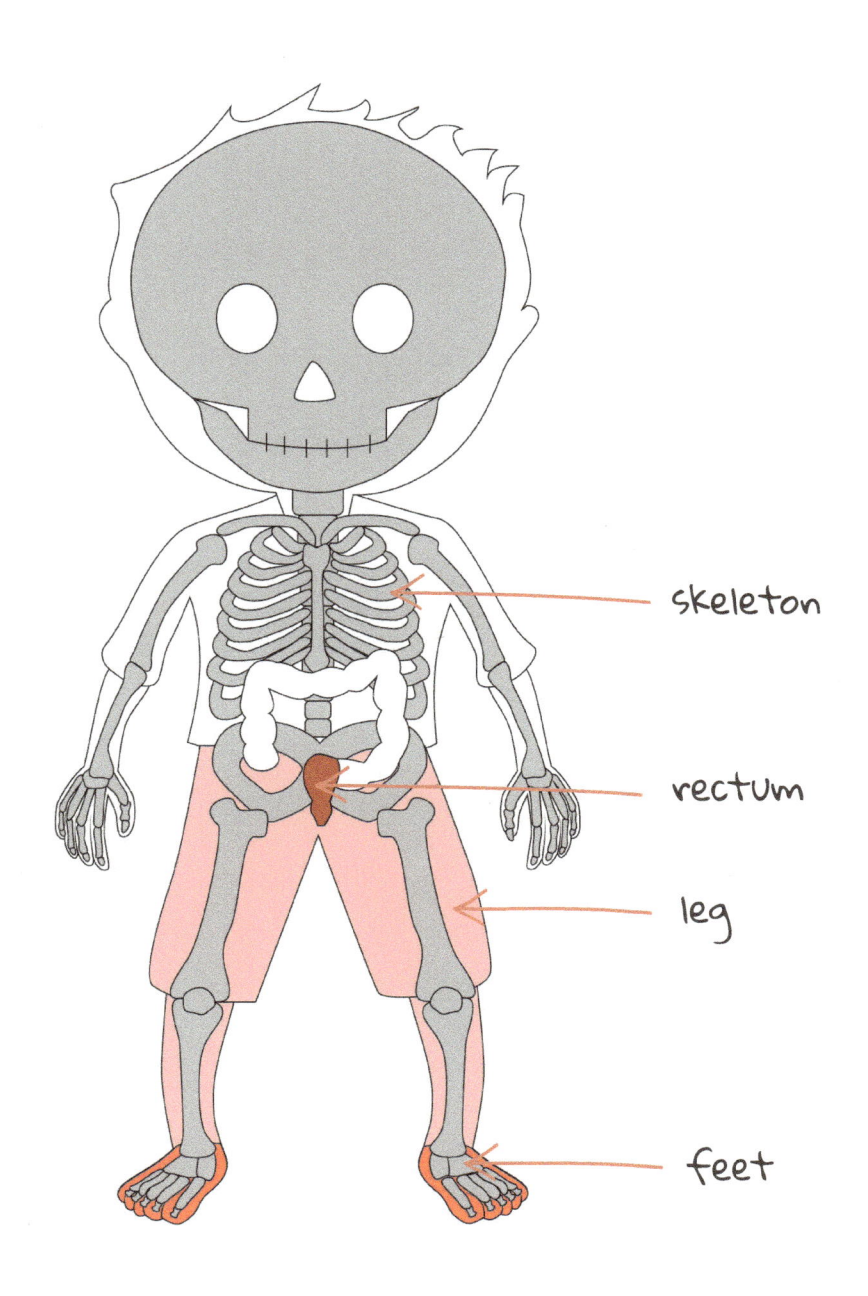

rectum

leg

feet

Body Mapping Your Feelings

FEET

Feel into your feet. Are they sore? Are they itchy? Maybe they are stinky?

If so I wonder what this might mean?

Sometimes you might feel stuck or you might be scared to take the first step when trying something new.

Sometimes you may not want to do the thing you are doing and be itching to do something else?

Maybe none of these have meaning ...?

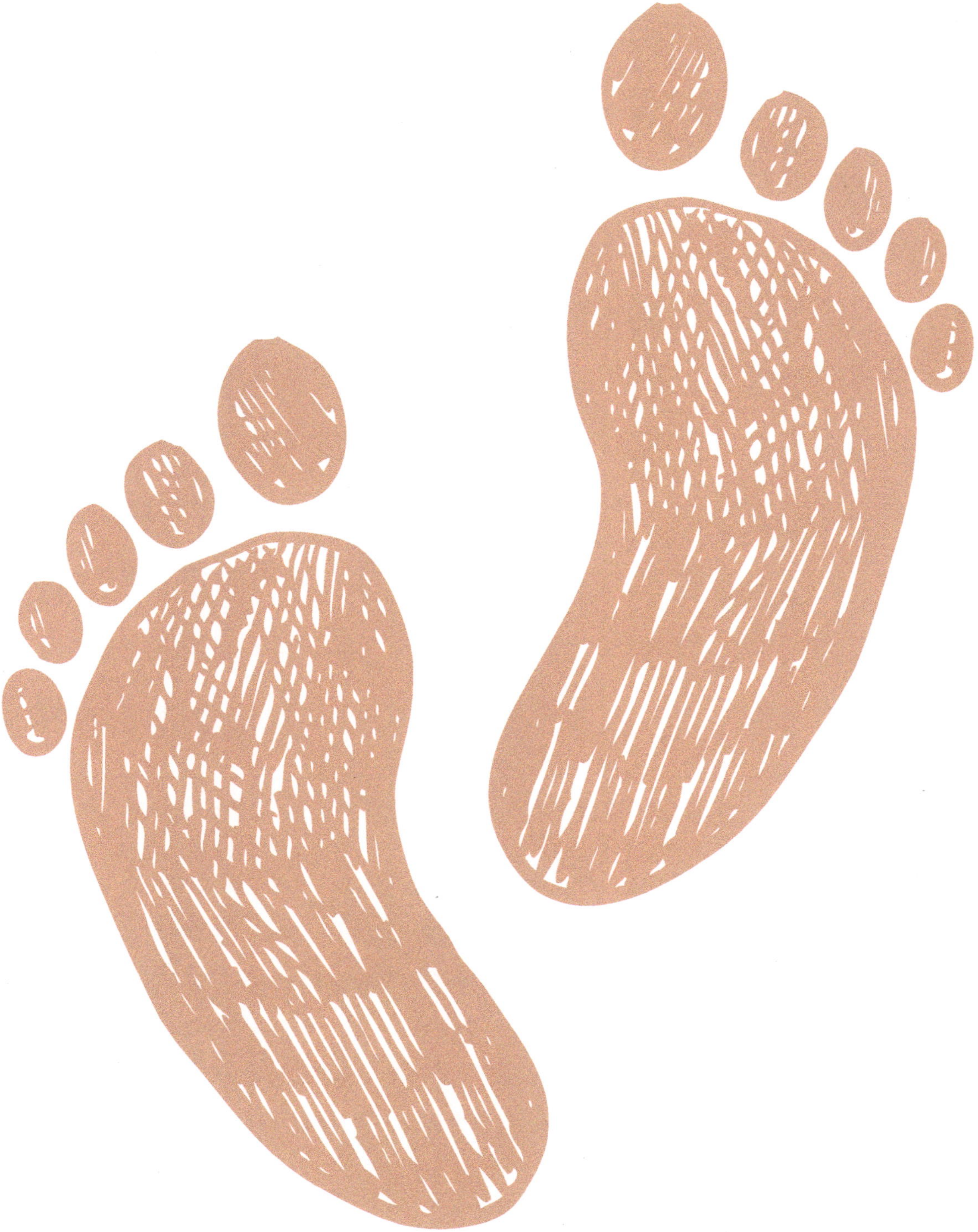

Ask your feet to tell you what they need?

Wiggle them, stamp them on the ground and send your attention and energy to your feet.

SENSING INTO YOUR FEET

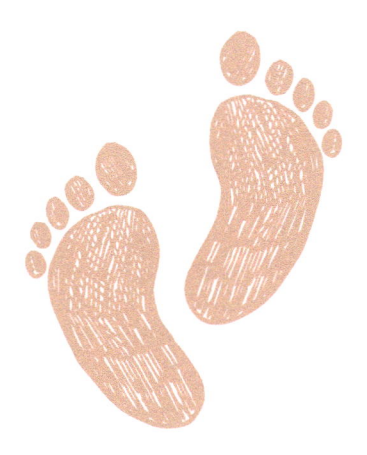

Write down what you feel on the next page.

You can also think about your other body parts in your Need to Be Safe and Secure, your legs, rectum and skeleton — look to the map of body parts on page 39. You might also sense into these parts and write down how these feel or might feel if you are not safe and secure.

I am safe

A Moment To Wonder

Imagine letting go of your concerns and worries knowing that all your needs are taken care of and that your needs matter.

Take a moment to position yourself like the girl and WONDER how it felt when you were safe in your Mother's womb.

When we put our body in certain positions it makes us feel safe.

Even if you don't remember being in your mother's womb your body does.

Write down or draw what this might feel like for you.

breathe

You can make yourself feel safe and secure anytime you want by connecting to your breath.

Breathe into the feelings of discomfort or unease in your body when you are scared, feel uncertain or begin to panic.

You don't need to have an answer as to why you are feeling what you are in this moment and you don't have to fix anything at all.

... just be in the wonder of YOU

FEEL all the FEELINGS that arise as prompts.
THESE ARE IMPORTANT MESSAGES.
You can do this at anytime, anywhere you are ...
YOU SAY THE WORDS BELOW

breathing in...
I calm my body
breathing out...
I relax

(Repeat these two sentences as
many times as you like)

I Can Affirm Myself

I AM	I AM
_____	_____

I AM	I AM
_____	_____

I am safe

I am worthy of having my needs met

My Tribe

Who's in your tribe?

We all need a tribe of people around us that will support us when we are not feeling safe and secure.

Sometimes when we are feeling a bit anxious it can be hard to remember who can help us.

WHO ARE three people that you can talk to about your feelings and needs and who will always support your growth.

1. ....

2. ....

3. ....

This is my tribe

Map Your Family's WONDER

Interview time

Do you ever wonder what life was like for your parents, grandparents or great-grandparents?

It is hard to think of your parents as children, you've only ever known them as grown-ups! But they were children once, feeling the same emotions as you, sharing similar experiences and seeking answers to the same questions as you.

INTERVIEWING an older family member can help you map the family's wonder. Who knows what you will discover!

Ask them to tell you about a time when they didn't feel safe or secure?

Record the answers

What did they do?

What was their body telling them?

After you have done the interview you can think back to what you need to be safe and secure ... and WONDER if this is something the grown-up you interviewed has felt too?

Natures Abundance

Experiencing nature helps us feel grounded — we can sink our feet in the sand or grass and imagine the powerful earth supporting us. We can think about the people who have walked in this exact place on earth before us and draw on their collective strength to feel secure.

Think about the amazing colours of a rainbow you see in the sky — red, orange, yellow, green, blue and indigo.

Now go on a treasure hunt and find items from nature that represent these colours — it can be leaves, flowers, grass, pebbles, sand, branches, herbs — anything that you find in nature. Bring all your treasure back and create your own beautiful rainbow using these items.

As you are creating your masterpiece, think about how nature provides for us throughout the seasons.

55

I like this about being in nature...

(Use this space to put a photo or draw or write about what nature means to you)

WORD SEARCH

```
Q X A B S K U S N T Y V
M X B B I E J B T E V I
W I I L A U C T S U R T
A S A F E L A U Z I N H
P G G N R R A I R J E E
B S I R A N T N F E B A
W P O D O S P U C Y Y L
Q G H O E U B B H E C T
A Q P R T Q N X C H D H
O L Q T M H Z D T A F Y
V X U Y N O E X E L F E
T H F A J G R Y W D O B
```

BALANCED
SECURE
TRUST
REST

SOOTHE
GROUNDED
SAFE
HEALTHY

My touchstone

When I am unsafe

I feel ....

I need ....

This soothes me and makes me feel safe and secure.

2. I am free

I am emotionally free

The second of your Foundational Needs is your 'Need to Feel'.

Every child needs to feel the full range of feelings and emotions in all of their experiences.

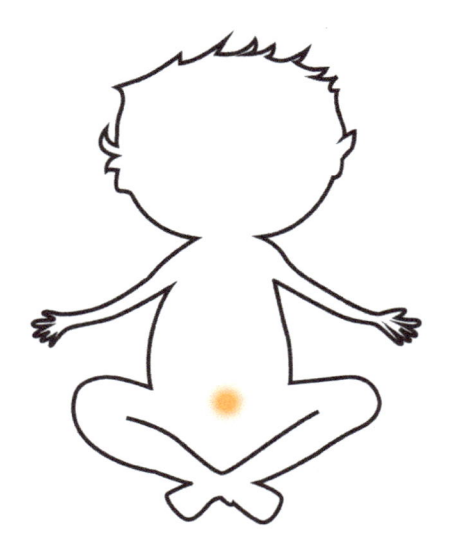

Sometimes you may not like what you feel. Sometimes you might be told the feelings you have are not appropriate. All of your feelings are important even if some are called negative and some positive.

You can move with more ease when you feel all of your feelings.

When we hold the idea that 'My feelings do not matter' or 'I don't like this feeling' we lose some rhythm and inner freedom and can get stuck.

Feeling stuck helps us to remember that we need to explore our deeper emotions and feelings and when we do this it leads to a full expression of life.

Imagine for yourself how emotionally free you are.

Can you...

- feel into the part of your body that feels stuck?
- talk about your feelings with words?
- draw or use another medium to express how you feel?
- be aware of your own feelings?
- know when someone else's feelings are not yours?
- find a way to regulate if you experience sensory overload?

If some of these things are hard to do, you can see how easily it would be to have a tantrum, feel out of control, stuck, or about to explode.

But when you know that these feelings all have important information about what you need, you learn how to flow through uncomfortable feelings when they arise.

I feel freedom when...

I know that it is ok for me to have sad feelings.
I am in water and swimming.
I know how to stop myself if I want something I can't have.
My parent or a teacher helps me to find words for my feelings.
I have time and space to feel all my feelings.
I can breathe easily and feel my body.
I know that these sad or hard feelings won't last.
I am out in nature and playing freely.
I am playing sport and games especially running.
I can scream and yell if I need to – without getting into trouble.
I can draw and create something.
The adults in my life are enjoying themselves.
I can move and dance.
People around me can help me understand my emotions.

Circle the ones that feel most true to you, you may find that you have a few.

write the things that make you feel emotionally free in and around the image

Free flowing feelings

confidence freedom creative

pleasure desire celebration

happy spontaneous joyful

sensory enjoyment enthusiastic

self-assured passionate

I feel free in my body when... ....

....

I feel happy in my body when... ....

....

I feel joyful in my body when... ....

....

Harder to move feelings

stuck
out of control
fussy
hypersensitive
jealous
inflexible
miserable
impulsive
uncertain
explosive
obsessive

I feel stuck in my body when... ....
....

I feel unhappy in my body when... ....
....

I feel miserable in my body when... ....
....

Listen to your body's wisdom

There will be times when you don't always feel free and this is when it is most important to trust your body so you can listen to what your body is telling you.

To listen to the body remember we SENSE with our whole body.

Your need to feel free is felt in the body locations of your hip area, reproductive system, urinary system, bladder, endocrine system, large intestine, pelvis and appendix.

See these highlighted on the next page.

colon
appendix
hip area
urinary system

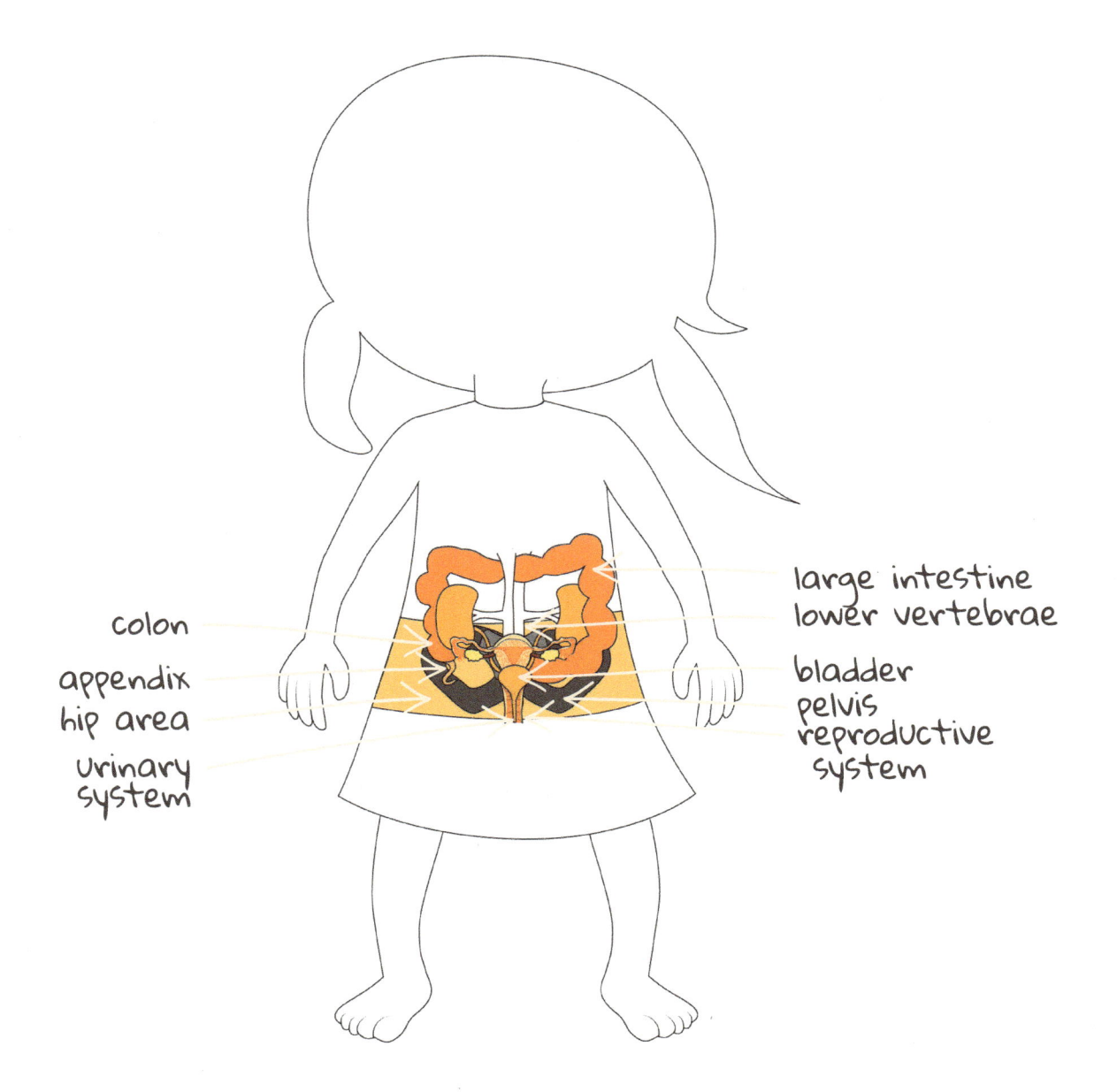

large intestine
lower vertebrae
bladder
pelvis
reproductive system

Body Mapping Your Feelings

HIP AREA

Feel into your hips. Are they wobbly? Are they stuck? Maybe they are sore?

If so I wonder what this might mean?

Sometimes you might feel you can't move freely and get stuck?

Sometimes you may have some jobs to do and just want to dance and play?

Maybe none of these have meaning ...?

73

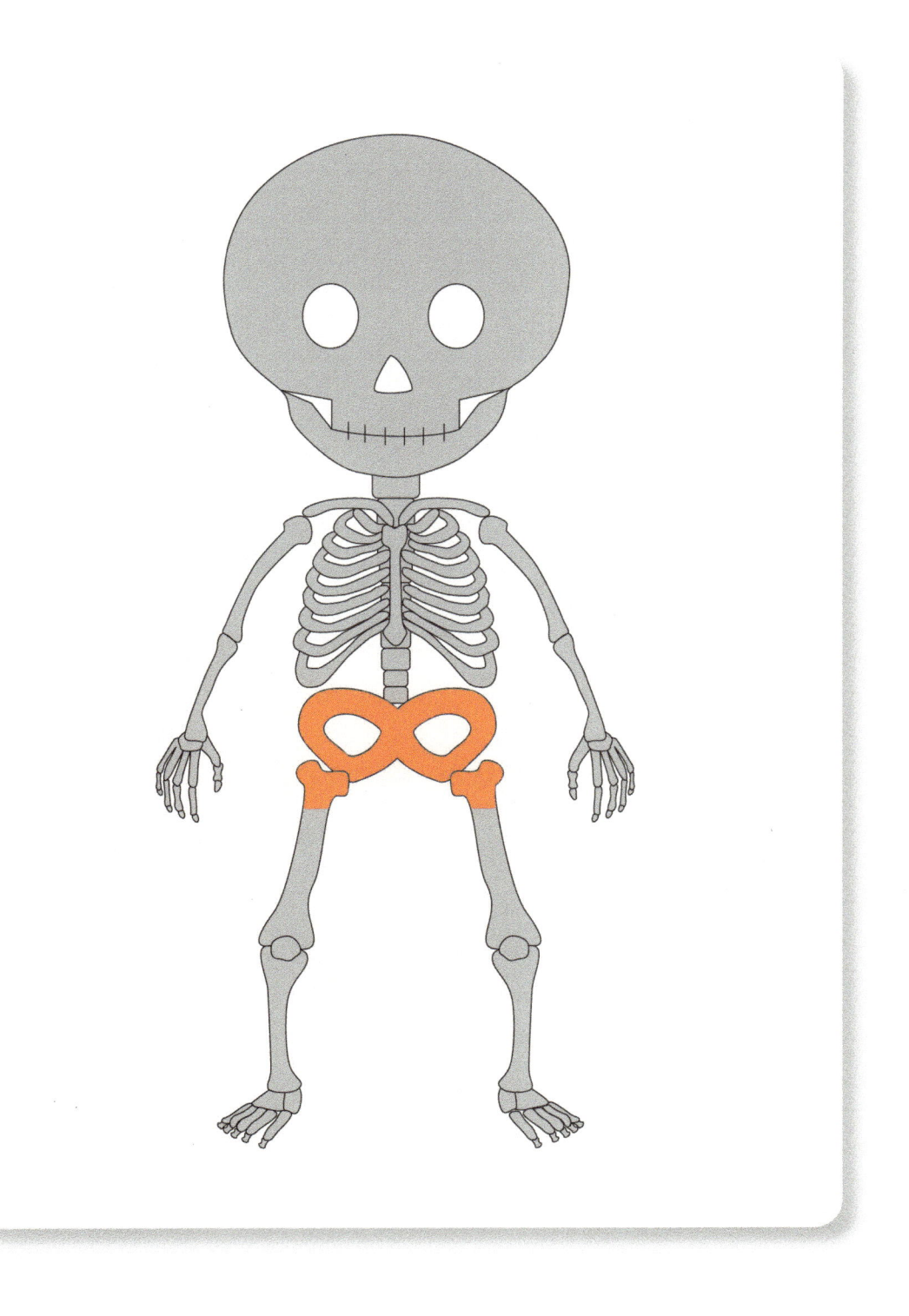

Ask your hips to tell you what they need?

Wiggle them, make pelvic circles moving your hips around and around, send your attention and energy to your hips.

SENSING INTO YOUR HIPS

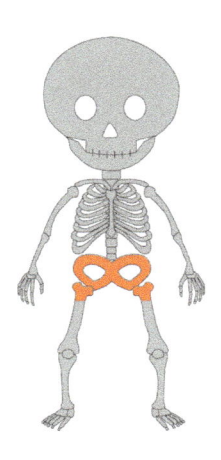

Write down what you feel on the next page.

You can also think about your other body parts in your Need to Feel, your reproductive system, urinary system, bladder, endocrine system, large intestine, pelvis, and appendix — look to the map of body parts on page 71. You might also sense into these parts and write down how these feel or might feel if you are not able to be free flowing with your emotions.

I am moved

I am in tune with the rhythm of my life

A Moment To Wonder

If you feel off balance with your emotions focus on what feels best for you.

Move your hips in a way that feels good for you, this can bring balance back into your body.

You can practice your inner balance anytime you like. If you feel sad move into the sadness in the same way you practice using a hula-hoop. Be in WONDER as your hips move around and around as you free up sadness and wonder what feeling pops up next.

As you do this you might like to say.

I move easily and effortlessly

I flow with life

breathe

You can make yourself feel free anytime you want by connecting to your breath.

Breathe into the feelings of discomfort or unease in your body when you note you are overwhelmed, impulsive or stuck.

You don't need to have an answer as to why you are feeling what you are in this moment and you don't have to fix anything at all.

... just be in the wonder of YOU

FEEL all the FEELINGS that arise as prompts.
THESE ARE IMPORTANT MESSAGES.
You can do this at anytime, anywhere you are ...
YOU SAY THE WORDS BELOW

breathing in...
I move my body

breathing out...
I feel at ease

(Repeat these two sentences as
many times as you like)

I am happiest when ...

Ride the wave of life and enjoy being happy.

I am happy

I celebrate my life

I have been
ignoring these feelings

and now I can
let them be felt...

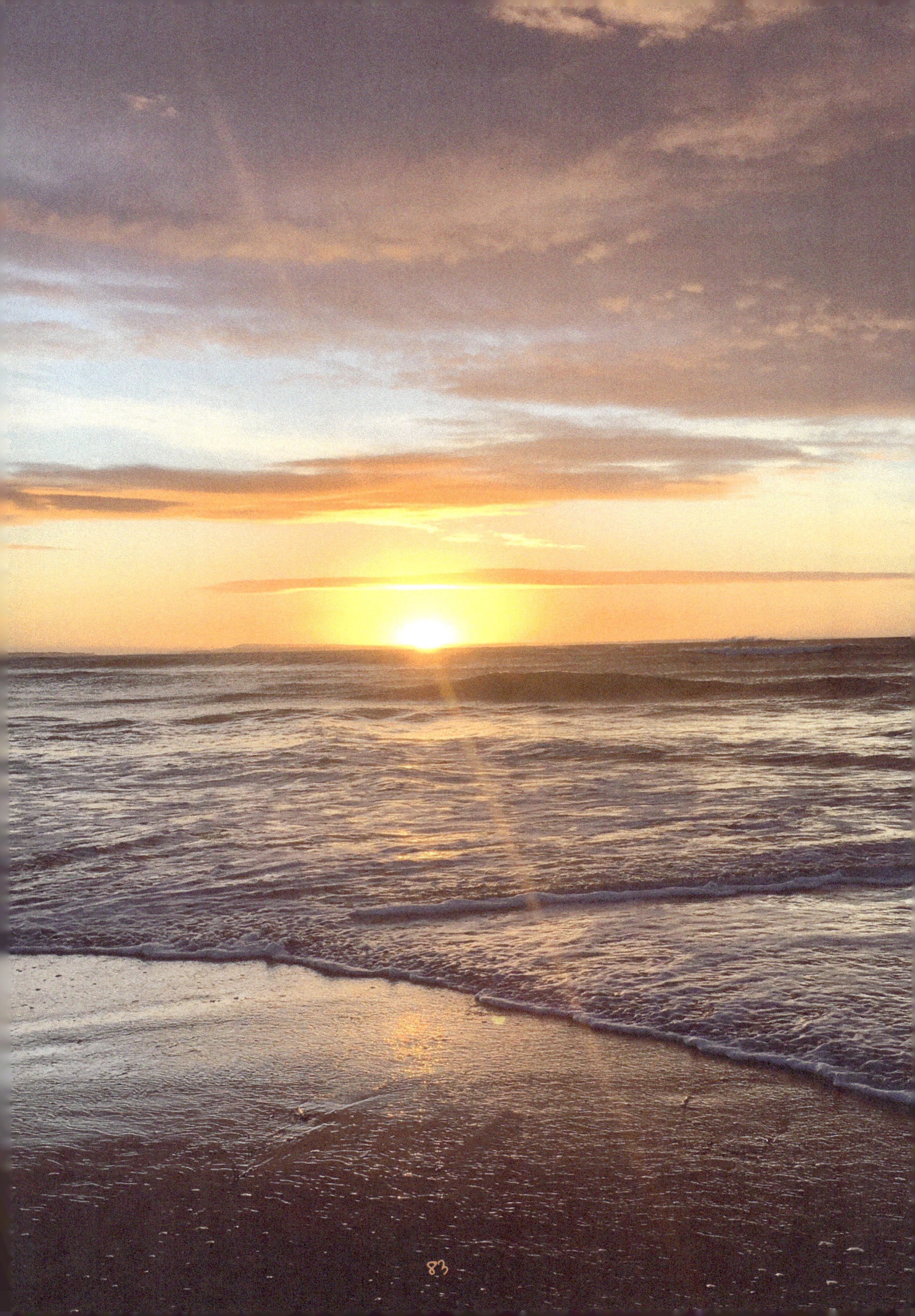

The places that make me feel a sense of freedom are ...

I like to be creative in this way ...

Let's get cooking

Do you know you have creative gifts and talents that are different to anyone else's?

Your special blend of unique talents is yours to enjoy.

In the same way you prepare the right ingredients to cook or prepare a certain type of food you need the ingredients of pleasure, joy and celebration for a creative life.

The energy you bring to anything you make is just as important as the ingredients you use.

If you feel inspired you might like to make these raw apricot and coconut balls to share with your family and friends.

And don't forget to share the unique ingredients that make up the WONDER OF YOU.

Apricot Wonder Balls

You will need:

1 cup of dried apricots chopped

1 cup of sultanas

1 cup of freshly squeezed orange juice

1 tbsp of grated orange rind

1 & 1/2 cups of shredded coconut

3/4 cup of cashews

+ 1/2 cup shredded coconut for rolling

To make:

Place the apricots, raisins, orange juice and orange rind in a small bowl. Cover the bowl and let it stand for one hour or overnight.

Place the mixture into a food processor and add the 1 & 1/2 cups of shredded coconut as well as all of the cashews.

Chop the mixture finely.

Take about 1 tbsp of the mixture and roll it into a ball.

Roll the ball in the remaining shredded coconut to cover it.

Repeat this process until all the balls are made.

Eat! These Apricot Wonder Balls can be stored in the fridge for up to 2 weeks.

Map Your Family's WONDER

Interview time

Ask an adult - a family member to tell you about a time when they felt sad or embarrassed about their feelings.

What was their body telling them?

What did they do?

Does your body communicate feeling sad or embarrassed in a similar way?

WORD SEARCH

```
U Z Y T I V I T A E R C
A E H C Z E Y H J Y O J
K E U U E R U S A E L P
Y E C N E D I F N O C W
L V N F Y A N E L A O L
B S E N S I T I V E K G
E N T H U S I A S M A K
K C E L E B R A T I O N
I N K M L R W W W Q R U
N S P O N T A N E I T Y
C Q B I O C V T O V H Z
X R F Y C Q H Q B U B T
```

PLEASURE   ENTHUSIASM
CONFIDENCE   SPONTANEITY
CELEBRATION   JOY
SENSITIVE   CREATIVITY

My touchstone

When I am stuck

I feel ....

I need ....

This frees me and makes me feel
I can cope with all my emotions.

3. I act

I act

I am allowed to be ME.

The third of your Foundational Needs is your 'Need to Act'.

Every child needs to be allowed to Act in accord with their own direction.

YOU know what is best for you and your growth.

How you act in the world is a wonderful indication of the feelings and thoughts you have. Once you can look beneath your action to the feelings and thoughts that created it, you can change the behaviour.

Sometimes your behaviours are hard to understand and sometimes other people might not like the way you behave.

You might have difficulty doing certain things — every one does. When you know how powerful you are at your core you, can do things that have been hard in the past.

When you feel an alignment, which means that when your feelings and thoughts match — then your actions are the very best for you. This is living from your soul.

Imagine how you act toward yourself, others and life when you can.

- follow your own intuition.
- feel good about yourself and the world (we sometimes call this self esteem).
- follow your inner direction on the things that matter to you.
- know that you are respected and you also respect others.
- know that your parents and teachers are working with you and helping you be the best you can be.

If some of these things are not possible you can see how easily it would be to have to push harder to get to do what you want. Or you might think you have to fight in a way to get to do what you want.

But when these needs are met you feel you CAN, DO AND ACT in a strong and powerful way and you are centred, competent, and self motivated.

I feel in alignment when...

I can make choices of my own.

I get to decide on what to wear.

I don't get in trouble for saying what I want or need.

I have time to get ready in my own way.

I am out in nature and hiking.

I am reassured that it is okay for me to do something.

I just know something is the right thing for me.

I can do something after I have felt I could not.

When I am reassured rather than put down.

I keep trying and do something that has been hard before.

I am allowed to do things on my own.

If I know I get to do something fun after I have done something hard.

I am part of a team and we have the same goal.

I know that I don't have to compete (and its ok if I win or lose).

Circle the ones that feel most true to you, you may find that you have a few.

write the things that make you feel aligned in and around the image

Strengthening feelings

balanced
courage
confidence
respect
self-esteem
powerful
responsibility
discipline
honour
motivated
self-acceptance
enough
independence
resilience

I feel great in my body when... ....

....

I feel powerful in my body when... ....

....

I feel good enough in my body when... ....

....

Weakening feelings

unbalanced
indecisive
discipline
self-defeating
disrespect
dominating
victimised
lack of confidence
co-dependence
low self-esteem
shame
cowardice
unmotivated

I feel self defeated in my body when... ....
....

I feel disrespected in my body when... ....
....

I feel not good enough in my body when... ....
....

Listen to your body's wisdom

There will be time when you don't always feel you can act or be powerful so it is important to trust your body and listen to what your body is telling you.

To listen to the body, remember we SENSE with our whole body.

Your Need to Act is felt in the body locations of your abdomen, stomach and digestive system, adrenal glands, upper intestine, liver, gall bladder, kidneys, pancreas, spleen.

See these highlighted on the next page.

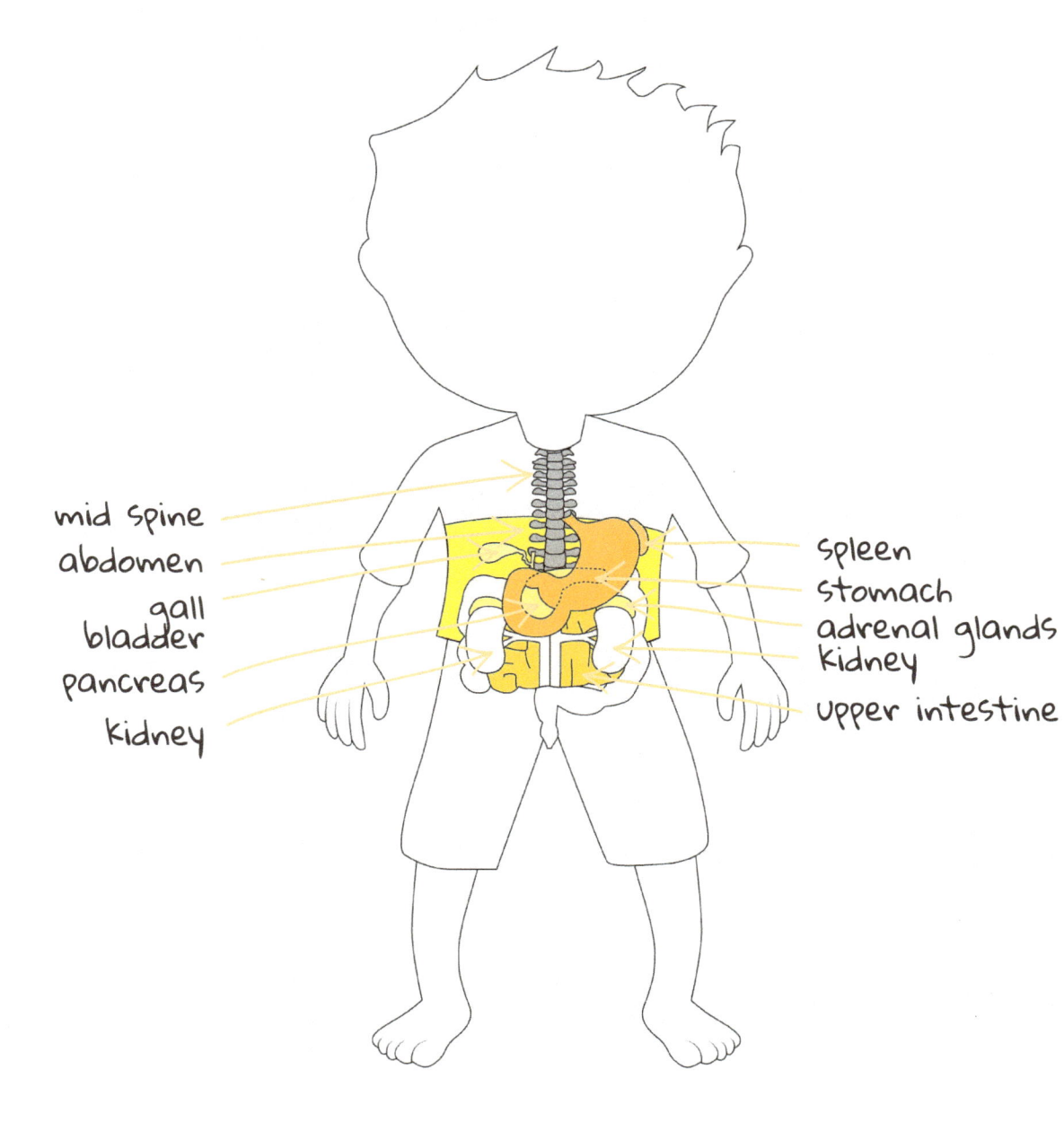

mid spine
abdomen
gall bladder
pancreas
kidney

spleen
stomach
adrenal glands
kidney
upper intestine

Body Mapping Your Feelings

STOMACH

Feel into your stomach.

Is it tight? Is it fluttery? Is it sickly?

If so, I WONDER what this might mean?

Perhaps you might feel that something is hard to stomach.

Do you have any upsets about a situation you are in?

Do you ever get a stitch, a cramp or a funny feeling in your tummy?

Maybe none of these have meaning …?

105

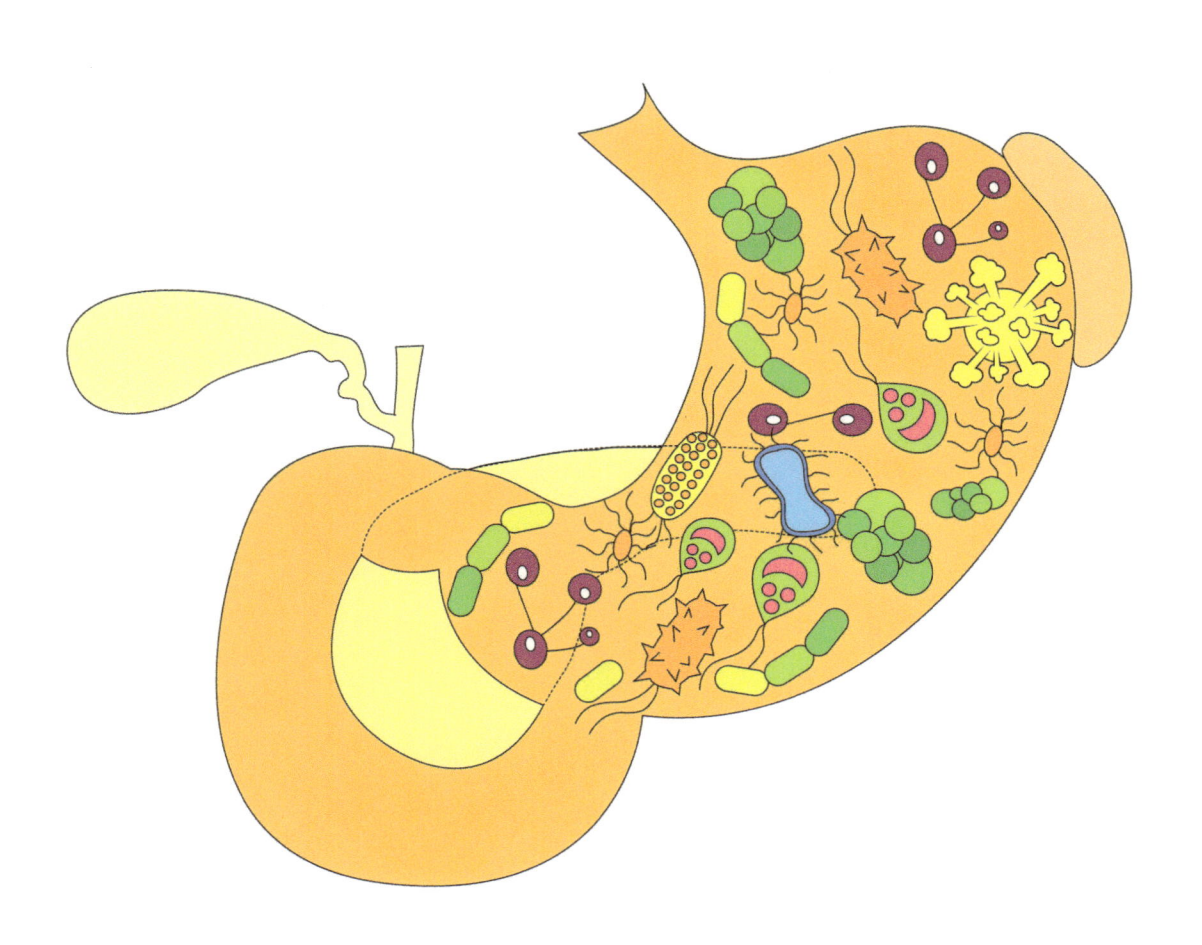

Ask your stomach to tell you what it needs?

Rub it gently, send your attention to your stomach. When you're hungry your body tells you — you can make sure the food you eat is good for your body. Pay attention when you are eating as you direct positive energy in your stomach. The body's microorganism's need a special environment to thrive, maybe you would like to learn more about this. This is called nutrition.

SENSING INTO YOUR STOMACH

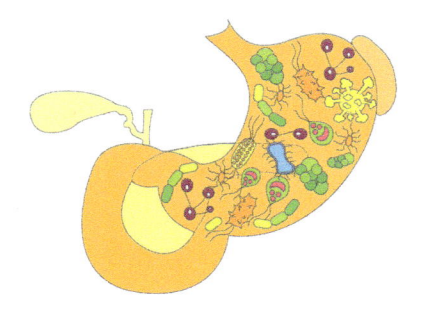

Write down what you feel on the next page.

You can also think about your other body parts in your Need to Act, your abdomen, digestive system, adrenal glands, upper intestine, liver, gall bladder, kidneys, pancreas, spleen — look to the map of the body parts on page 103. You might also sense into these parts and write down how these feel or might feel if you are not able to act.

108

A Moment To Wonder

Take a moment see what this boy sees from where he stands on the cliff.

Imagine being able to act on your inner guidance.

I WONDER how this boy feels to have so much in front of him to explore.

When you ask your body to show you the way you might find that it really does surprise YOU.

Feel how your body feels when you allow it to lead the way.

breathe

You can feel powerful anytime you want by connecting to your breath.

Breathe into the feelings of discomfort or unease in your body when you are feeling unmotivated, indecisive, uncertain, or ashamed.

You don't need to have an answer as to why you are feeling what you are in this moment and you don't have to fix anything at all.

... just be in the wonder of YOU

FEEL all the FEELINGS that arise as prompts.
THESE ARE IMPORTANT MESSAGES.
You can do this at anytime, anywhere you are ...
YOU SAY THE WORDS BELOW

breathing in...
I fill my body with life force (power)

breathing out...
I direct this power into my action

(Repeat these two sentences as many times as you like)

I CAN do these things ...

I am inspired

I allow my will to lead the way

When I'm aligned
with my
SOUL
I AM WHOLE
Body-Mind-Spirit
The way I Feel-Think-Act
is all together

When I have trouble doing something I can say or do these things to support my best actions.

1

2

3

Map Your Family's WONDER

Interview time

Ask an adult - a family member or elder to tell you how they feel when they are part of a group, when everyone is working together?

What is their body telling them?

Does your body communicate being part of a group in a similar way?

Now ask them how they feel when they are working on something just for them being focused on some project of their own.

What is their body telling them?

Does your body communicate being self-directed in a similar way?

WORD SEARCH

```
N H C I R Y O P T T P O
S B O N I G Y B L R J R
V V U D S P Q C U U E F
Q S R E K Q D O Y W X U
A P A P W M N J O P F Y
U R G E E O X P A M A E
T I E N H Y O P I J C K
O D A D Y B D T G T T M
N E R E K P P I J M U T
O B A N S G L L I W X S
M S B C R G R Z P B A O
Y C E E I J Y V B I L R
```

HONOUR
INDEPENDENCE
PRIDE
AUTONOMY

WILL
POWER
ACT
COURAGE

My touchstone

When I am ready to give up

I feel ....

I need ....

This strengthens me and keeps me open to achieving.

4.
I am love

I am love and I am loved

The fourth of your Foundational Needs is your 'Need to Love'.

Every child needs to be loved and to feel love for self and others.

YOU know how you need to be loved.

The Need to Love is about belonging and seeking loving relationships with YOU, your friends and family and others, as well as animals, plants, natural environments, and the whole of the world.

The feeling YOU get when you feel lovable is wonderful!

Imagine for yourself how lovingly you feel about yourself and life when you can know and show kindness.

- Be grateful for all people, places and things.

- Feel connected by love in your family — and extended and blended families.

- When you know that you don't have to do anything to be loved.

- When you know that you will be loved unconditionally.

If some of these things are not possible you can see how easily it would be to feel sad, get angry, sorrowful or hurt.

But when these needs are met you are kind, caring, grateful, compassionate, peaceful and in harmony.

I feel loved and loving when...

I ask for help and it's not a problem.

I am with my pets.

Someone does something kind for me.

Someone shares his or her things with me.

When someone notices that I am sad and asks if I need help.

I am with my friends.

I'm in the garden planting with my mum.

I get a hug in the morning.

When it's my birthday.

I get to do something I really love.

My brother/sister and I are not fighting.

Someone says nice things about me to others.

I have some time for love every day.

Circle the ones that feel most true to you, you may find that you have a few.

write the things that make you feel loved and loving in and around the image

Loving feelings

self-love respectful

open patient caring

gentle forgiving warm

soft compassionate

empathy kind grateful

I feel like I belong in my body when... ....
....
I feel peaceful in my body when... ....
....
I feel caring in my body when... ....
....

Unloving feelings

mean
impatient
rough
disrespectful
hard
dismissive
closed
self-absorbed
cruel
cold
angry

I feel closed or cold in my body when... ....
....

I feel rough and angry in my body when... ....
....

I feel cruel to others when... ....
....

Listen to your body's wisdom

Sensing with your whole body, feel into your Need to Love.

The Body locations for your Need to Love are your Heart, circulation, respiration (breathing) ribs, lungs, diaphragm, thymus arms and hands.

See these highlighted on the next page.

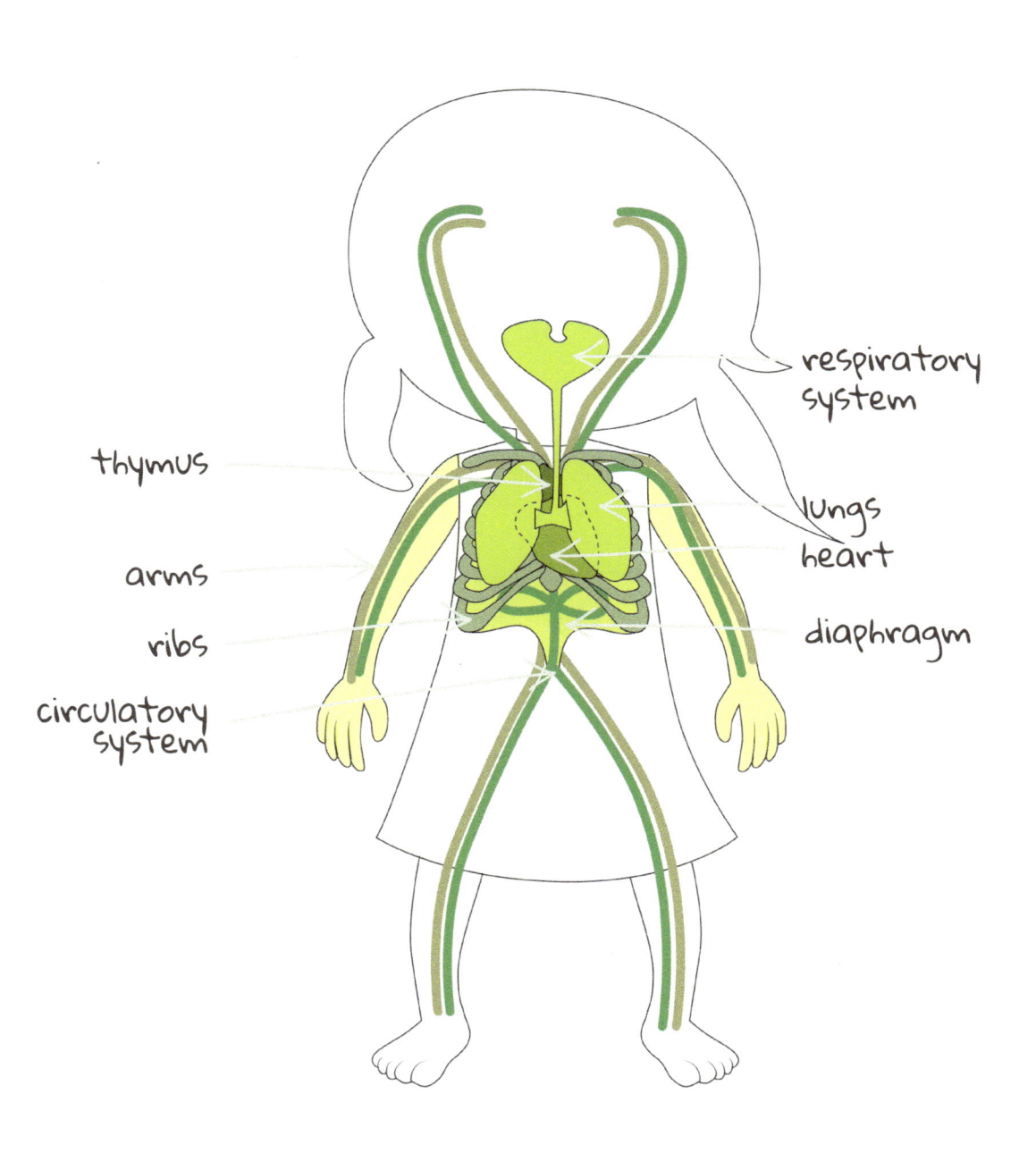

- respiratory system
- thymus
- lungs
- arms
- heart
- ribs
- diaphragm
- circulatory system

Body Mapping Your Feelings

HEART

Feel into your heart. Is it beating fast or slow? Is it sore? Is it jumpy? Is it quiet?

If so, I wonder what this might mean?

Sometimes you might feel tight and constricted and protecting your heart or sometimes you feel that your heart is so big — you wonder how it fits in your body.

Sometimes you may not like the way you feel in your heart as it hurts so much you want to cry.

Maybe none of these have meaning ...?

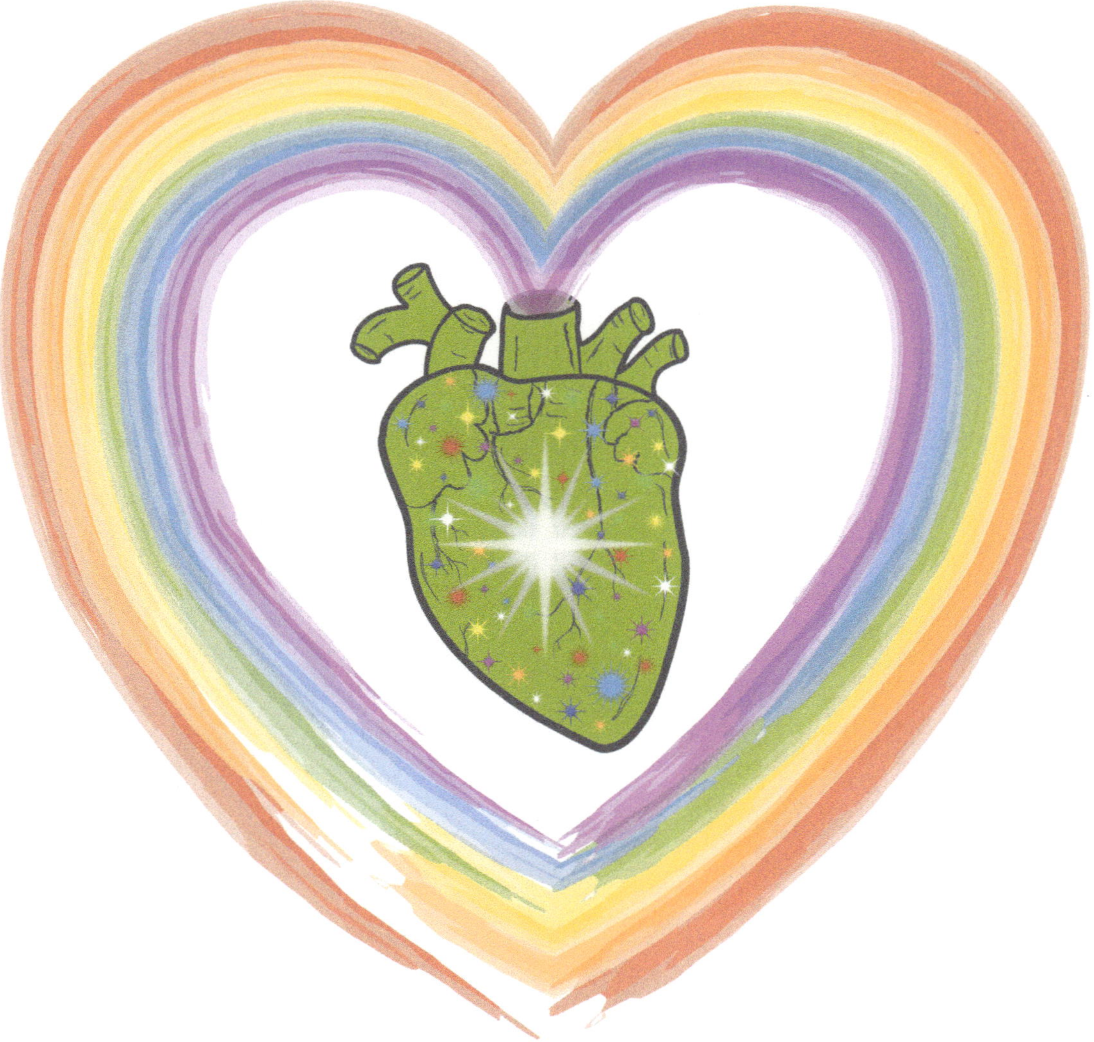

Ask your heart to tell you what it needs?

Feel your heart inside your body. Put both hands over your heart, which is located on the left hand side of your body

SENSING INTO YOUR HEART

Write down what you feel on the next page.

You can also think about your Need to Love as you sense into your circulatory system, respiratory system, lungs, ribs, diaphragm, arms and hands. You might also sense into these parts and write down how these feel or might feel if you are not feeling loved or loving.

136

A Moment To Wonder

Close your eyes and picture yourself filled with love.

Remembering the different feelings of love listed on the loving words page and see if you connect to these feelings of love.

Think of someone who loves you.

Think of someone you love.

Think of all the mothers throughout the generations of your family loving their children.

Do you feel the love in your heart and body?

You are LOVED!

breathe

You can make yourself feel loving anytime you want by connecting to your breath.

Breathe into the feelings of unease in your body when you note you are scared, angry or feel uncertain or panic.

You don't need to have an answer as to why you are feeling what you are in this moment and you don't have to fix anything at all.

... just be in the wonder of YOU

FEEL all the FEELINGS that arise as prompts.
THESE ARE IMPORTANT MESSAGES.
You can do this at anytime, anywhere you are ...
YOU SAY THE WORDS BELOW

breathing in...
I welcome love in

breathing out...
I send love out

(Repeat these two sentences as
many times as you like)

What a pet might need to be LOVED

Think about your pet or a pet you would love to have. What would your pet need in order to feel LOVED?

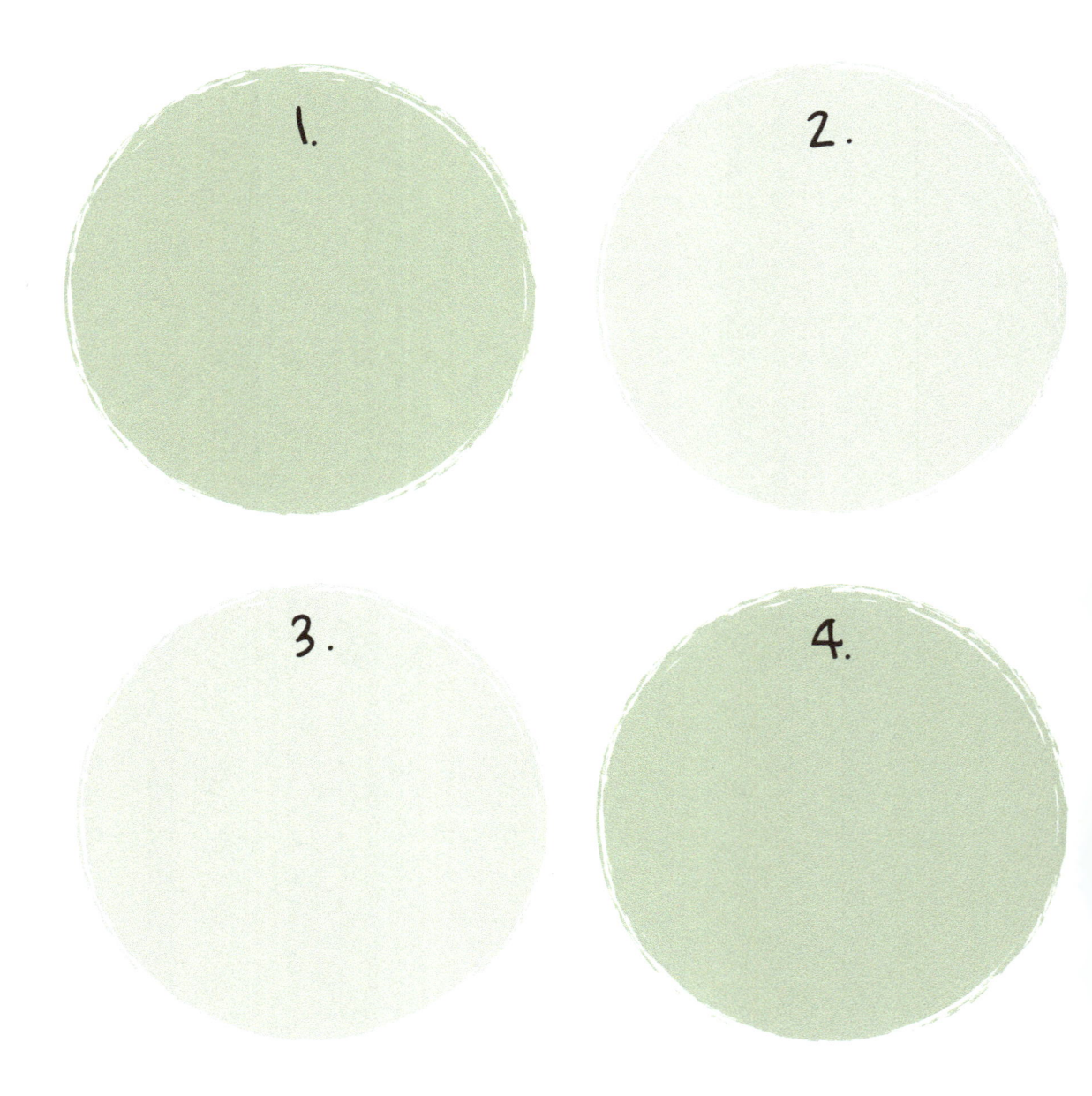

1.

2.

3.

4.

I am caring

I care for others how i like to be cared for

These things I love about me ....

These things I love about others ....

I AFFIRM LOVE when I AM loving
to myself and others.

I am loving

I love connecting with myself and others

Gratitude beads

When we focus on the people, places and things that we are grateful for, our hearts open wider and support our need to love.

Many religions, tribes and cultures around the world practice Gratitude. Gratitude is another way of giving thanks and creates harmony and peace in our hearts and lives.

Gratitude beads are a beautiful way to remind us to be grateful every day. Hold them in your hands and touch each bead. As you do, say one thing you are grateful for. Repeat the process until you have touched each of the ten beads and said the ten things you are grateful for that day.

To make your own gratitude beads you will need:

- A piece of ribbon or string
- A tassel
- 10 beads
- A charm you love

Start by securing the tassel at one end of the string – ask a grown-up to help you tie a secure knot.

Thread each bead onto the string. When all the beads are on, add the charm and tie another knot – you may need to ask a grown-up for help again!

Carry these beads with you every day and when you touch them, you will be reminded of all the things in your life that you are grateful for.

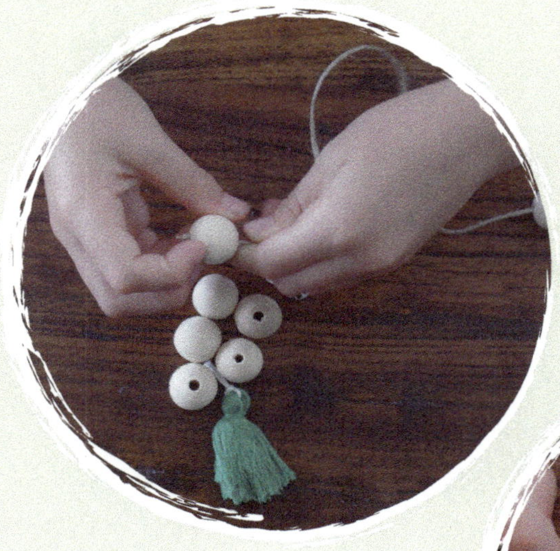
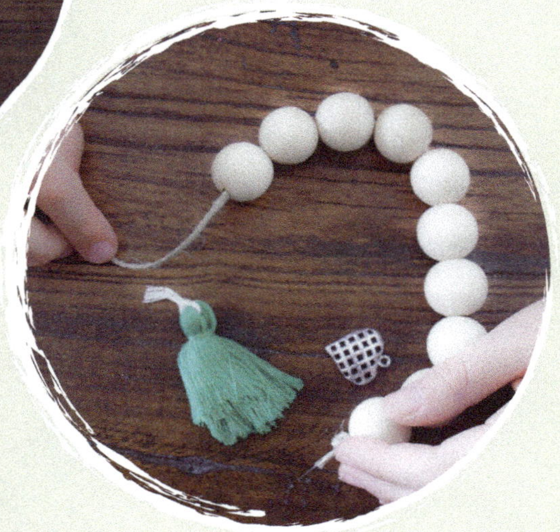
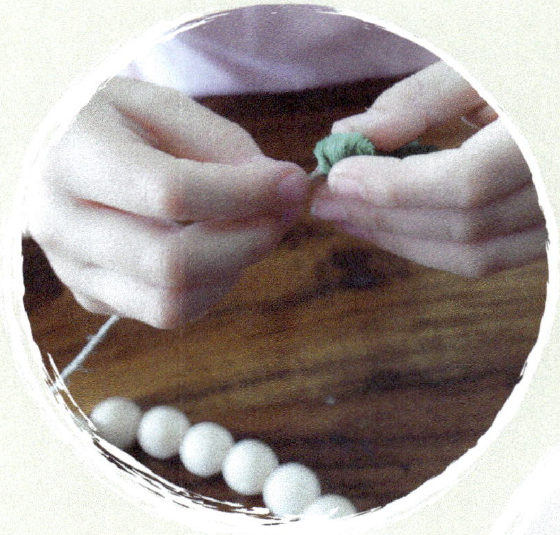
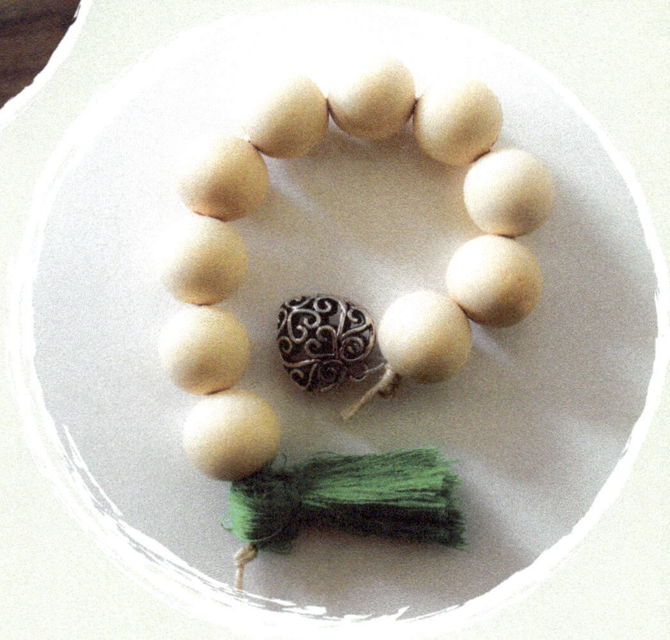

Map Your Family's WONDER

Interview time

Ask a family member, a brother or sister, a parent or an aunt or uncle help you map the family's wonder about the need to love and be loved.

Who knows what you will discover!

Ask them to tell you about a time when they didn't feel loved by someone in the family and they felt isolated from the rest of the family – like they did not belong?

Record the answers.

What did they do?

What was their body telling them?

After you have done the interview you can think back to what you need to be loved and loving ... and WONDER if this is something the family member you interviewed has felt too.

WORD SEARCH

```
Q L O V I N G Y Q I B J
W A Y N C E G K B E V L
K Y C N J N I Q M F D J
Y S A B I I Y Z S N R A
C O B R A H B D I E M E
J I A Q T T G K S H Q B
X H D A H H B Z I C I H
S V P Z I P E A C E X N
K M Y P N D C S M K I G
E A F F E C T I O N Q A
N H B L K I E R A C T M
I B P Q E C I V R E S J
```

LOVING   AFFECTION

EMPATHY   PEACE

SERVICE   KIND

CARE   SHARING

My touchstone

When I am angry

I feel ....

I need ....

This softens me and makes me feel open to be more loving.

5.
I speak

I speak

The fifth of your Foundational Needs is your 'Need to Speak'.

Every child needs to speak about what matters to them and to be heard.

YOU have so much to say.

The need to speak is all about listening, hearing and speaking. Even if someone does not use words, they are still communicating in other ways it just means we have to pay more attention and listen to what they are conveying.

Sometimes you may feel heard and appreciated for your words. And other times it's like no one is listening or no one wants to pay you any attention. Sometimes you may not feel like speaking or talking and sometimes you will feel like talking a lot.

Imagine for yourself how much you can speak up and communicate what you need.

Can you...

- tell others how you feel about something that bothers you?
- speak clearly and with certainty about what matters to you?
- find a different way to say or communicate the same thing if someone has not heard you?
- listen and wait until everyone has expressed in the group before you jump in?

If some of these things are not possible to feel you can see how easy it would be to close down from talking and go silent, to yell to try and get heard, or to make up a story that feels more exciting because you are nervous you are not getting noticed.

But when the Need to Speak is met you have a very clear voice, express yourself, speak wisely truthfully, and authentically.

Your voice allows you to tell others around you what you need and how you feel.

I wonder how it feels to take turns to listen to others – open and let them express their needs and feelings as well.

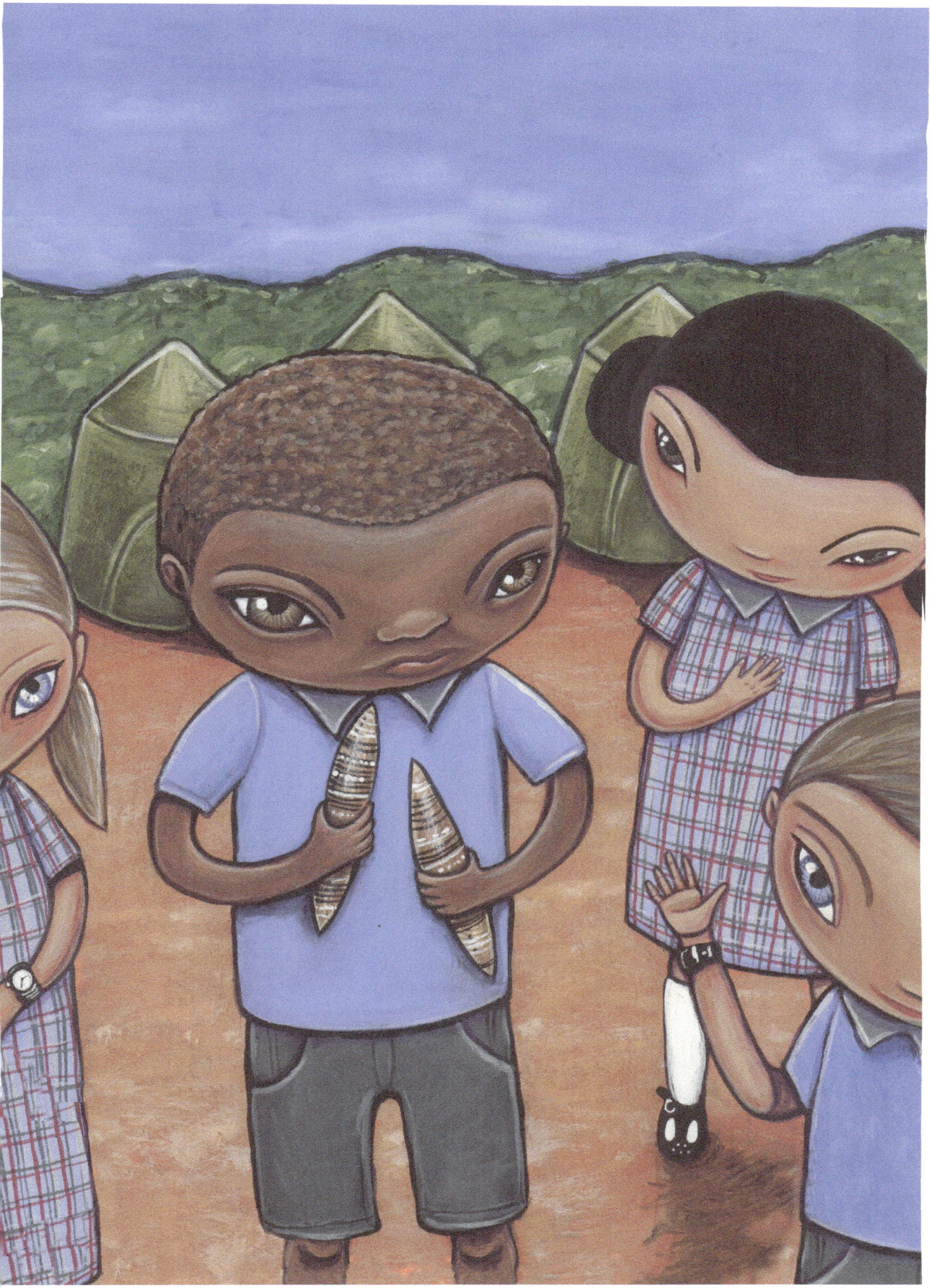

I can speak and I am heard when ...

I can say what I need to say.

The people I am talking to listen closely.

The person talking to me uses my name and looks at me.

I am reassured that it is okay for me to talk.

I am not interrupted by anyone.

I am given the space to find the words before someone does the talking for me.

I am informed truthfully and there are no secrets or lies.

I go to grandmas, as I know she listens to me.

There is a common interest to talk about between us.

I write poetry or music or write in my diary or journal.

When I know I won't get in trouble for saying something I feel.

The other children I'm talking with don't laugh or make fun of me.

I feel the person I talk to will keep it in confidence — they won't tell anyone else.

Circle the ones that feel most true to you, you may find that you have a few.

write the things that you need to speak up and be heard

High vibration speech

truth   authenticity   wisdom

open voice   clear speech

appreciative

confident   gentle tone

resonance   honesty

open listening   creativity

I feel clear to express my voice when... ....
....

I feel authentic and truthful when... ....
....

I feel I can express myself creatively when... ....
....

Lower vibration speech

shaky   invisible   lying

frustrated   inauthentic

Whispering and excluding others

stuttering   muffled voice

dismissing   yelling

I feel invisible to others when… ……………………………………………
……………………………………………………………………………………………
I feel inauthentic when… ……………………………………………………
……………………………………………………………………………………………
I feel my voice shut down when… …………………………………………
……………………………………………………………………………………………

Listen to your body's wisdom

There will be time when you don't always feel that you can speak up or be heard by others so it is important to trust your body and listen to what your body is telling you.

Remember when we listen to our body we are SENSING with our whole body.

Your Need to Speak is felt in the body locations of your throat, mouth, teeth, gums and lymphatic system.

See these highlighted on the next page.

hypothalamus	
	teeth
gums	trachea
mouth	esophagus
neck vertebrae	tongue
thyroid	parathyroid
thymus	bone marrow
lymphatic system	spleen

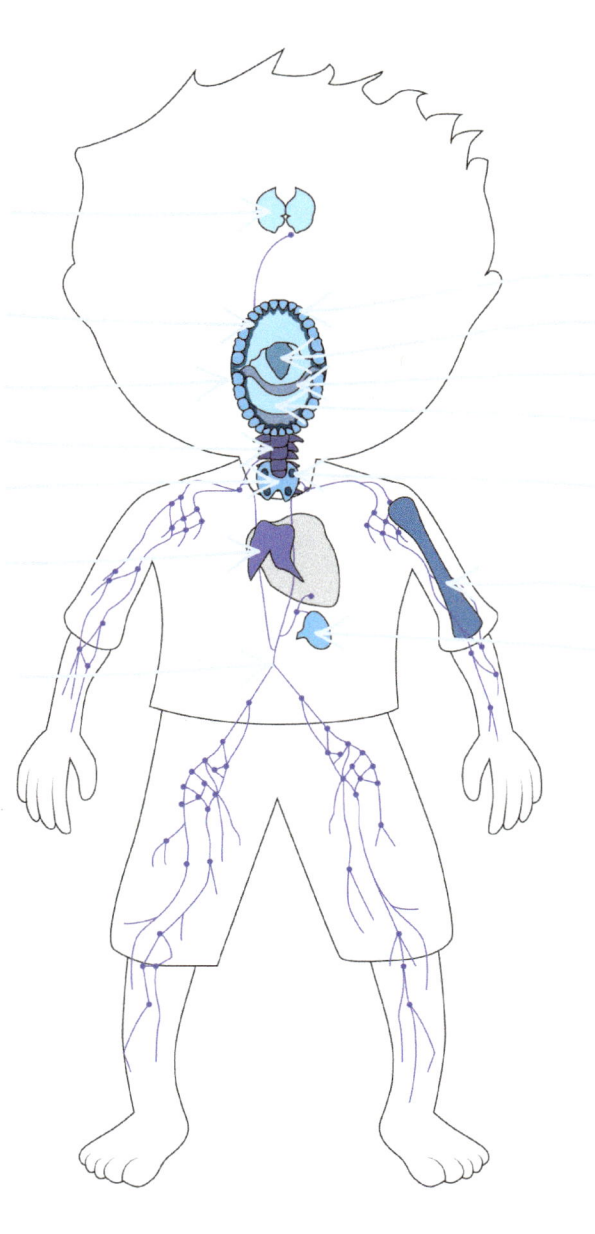

Body Mapping Your Feelings

TEETH

Feel into your teeth. Are they strong?
Are they closed together or open?
Do you have gaps in your teeth?
Is your jaw clenched tight?

If so, I wonder what this might mean?

Do you ever feel that something is hard to chew,
bite down on, or chomp?

Do you get a funny sensation when you
eat something cold?

Do you have a toothache?

Maybe none of these have meaning …?

165

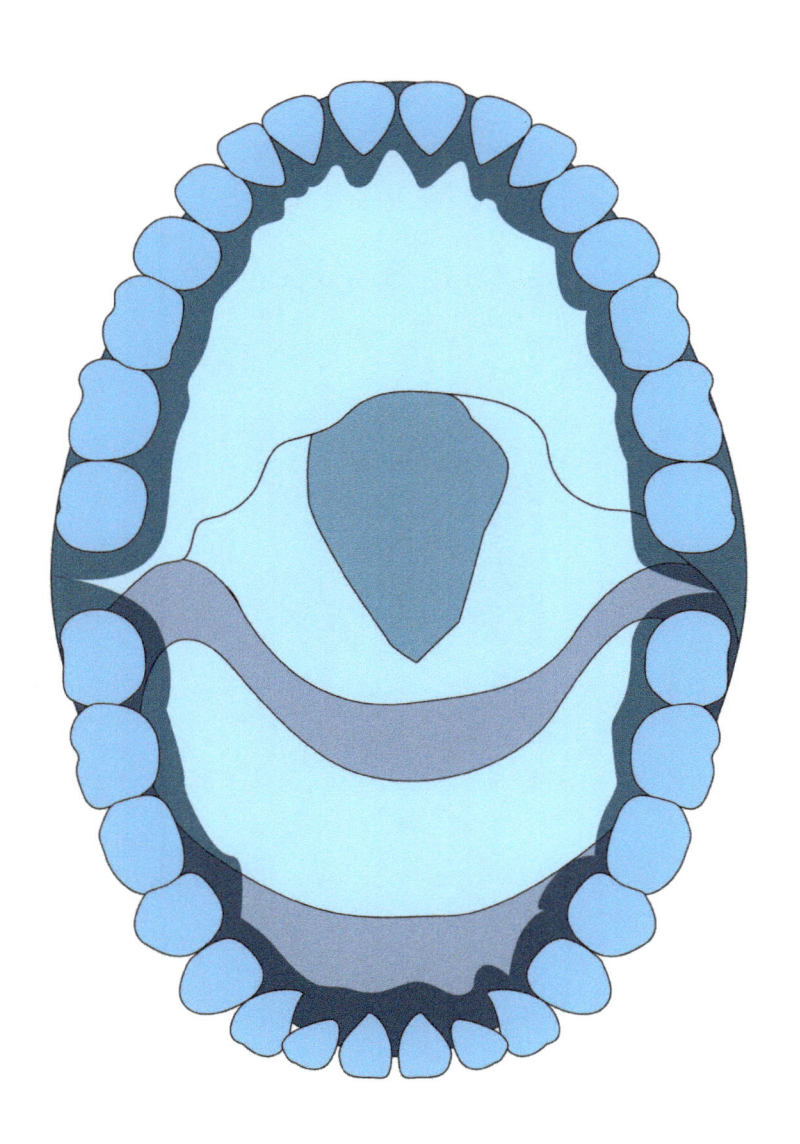

Ask your teeth to tell you what they need?

Run your tongue over your teeth and see if they are smooth or bumpy.

Do you have all your teeth? Have you lost some of your baby teeth?

Do any teeth have a special meaning?

SENSING INTO YOUR TEETH

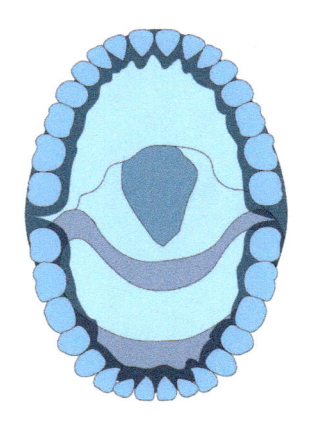

Write down what you feel on the next page.

You can also think about your other body parts in your Need to Speak, your throat, mouth, teeth and gums, lymphatic system, thyroid, thymus, hypothalamus, esophagus, spleen — look to the map of body parts on page 163. You might also sense into these parts and write down what you feel when you are not heard or able to speak.

I am original

Creativity flows in and around me

A Moment To Wonder

Think about something you have trouble talking about, or someone that you want to talk to but don't feel you are heard.

Take a moment to reach out and imagine that you are scooping up the energy that surrounds you. The swirling energies of numbers, colours, ideas, sounds and vibrations are all flowing in and through you. You are a channel of energy that has to express itself someway to bring balance back into your body. Hold the energy you scoop up as long as you need and then when you are ready, let it go.

Maybe you want to write, draw or sing a song.

Maybe you are ready to tell someone something you have been holding onto.

And now you can express and let it go.

breathe

You can express yourself and your needs anytime you want by connecting to your breath.

Breathe into the feelings of discomfort or unease in your body when you note you are nervous, silenced, uncertain or shaky YOU might stutter.

You don't need to have an answer as to why you are feeling what you are in this moment and you don't have to fix anything at all.

... just be in the wonder of YOU

FEEL all the FEELINGS that arise as prompts.
THESE ARE IMPORTANT MESSAGES.
You can do this at anytime, anywhere you are ...
YOU SAY THE WORDS BELOW

breathing in...
I ready myself to express

breathing out...
I say what I need to say

(Repeat these two sentences as many times as you like)

Charades

Draw 4 pictures that tell a story.
Give clues to make it easy to see what story the pictures are saying. I WONDER if anyone can guess what the story is about? How close do their words match your story?

I am wise

I listen to others and speak the truth

How would you communicate with a person that is deaf?

How would you communicate with a person who doesn't speak?

How would you communicate with a person who speaks another language?

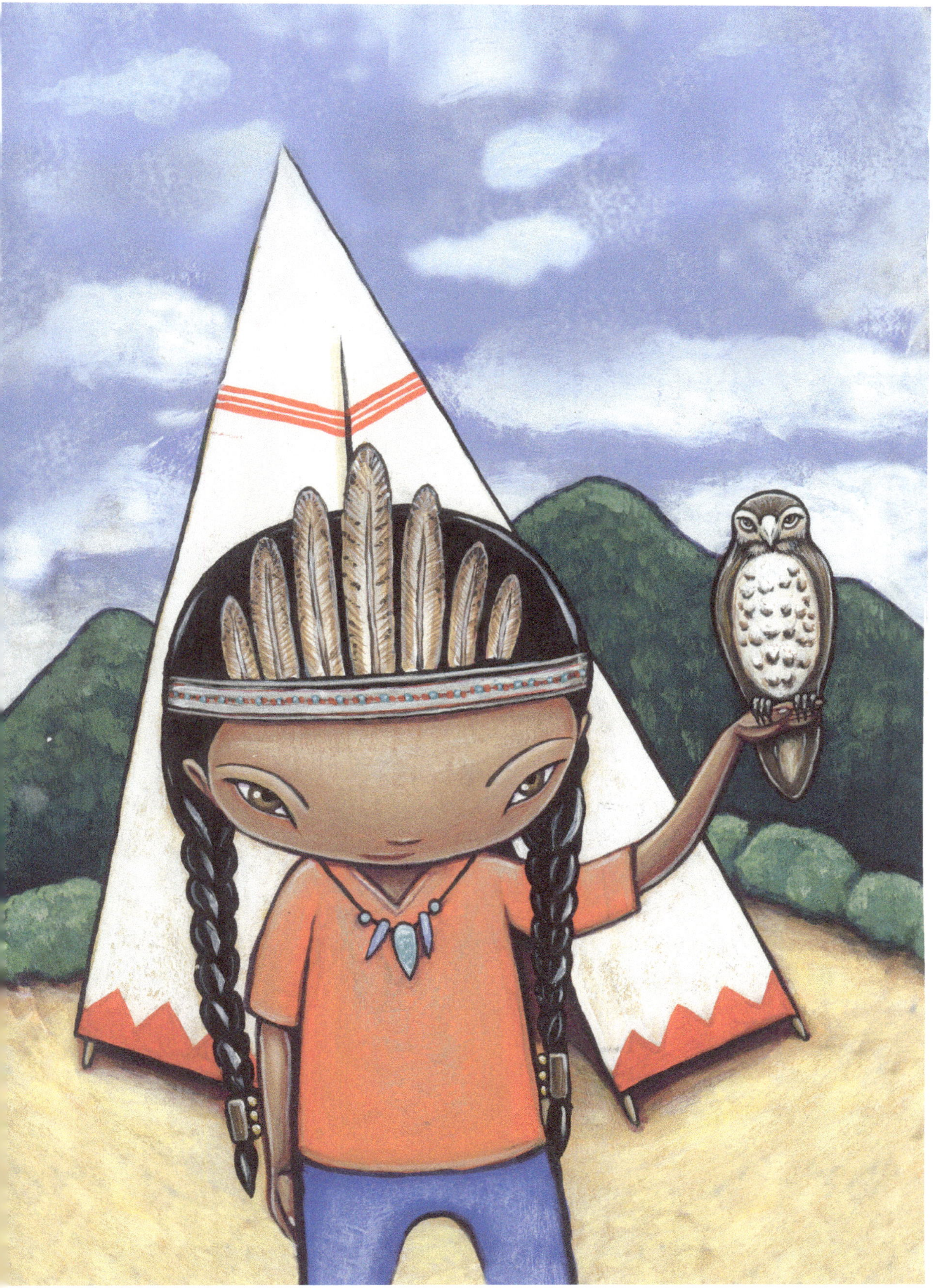

Map Your Family's WONDER

Interview time

Have you ever noticed that your family has sayings or words that other people don't say or might not understand?

Your family has a special type of language and the words we say in families give us clues about our ancestors.

Families with Jewish Decent might say
'Oh Vey' — when something is frustrating.
Families with Irish decent might say
'To be sure' — when they agree with something.

Ask your parents if they feel there are any words or phrases that have been passed down from their parents.

Are there any things that their parents said that they now say to you?

List all the words and sayings that are part of your family's language. Words or a phrase that might not have begun with your parents but came from someone else in the family and now it has carried over.

WORD SEARCH

```
V Q L Z F O R U Y M Z S
U T S V F P L I S J X Z
E X P R E S S I O N N G
G T E U R R V O I C E S
M H E G N I N E T S I L
D L C N R D I Q P I I J
B D H O R O X K X V J L
B P E W H V O U D S F R
J I A Z G N I R A E H Y
I I H K L A N G U A G E
A U T H E N T I C L W B
A H T U R T T L X O V J
```

SPEECH   EXPRESSION
AUTHENTIC   LANGUAGE
HEARING   VOICE
LISTENING   TRUTH

My touchstone

When I am ignored

I feel ……………………………………

I need ……………………………………

This supports me to feel heard.

6.
I imagine

I See

The sixth of your Foundational Needs is your 'Need to See'.

Every child needs to see, believe and imagine their best growth according to what they feel and think. What does the best version of you look like?
– Can you see it?

You have a special imagination that works in harmony with your dreams. It is important for you to imagine beyond what you see in front of you to bring into your life all those things you can see in your minds eye.

Dream Big.

YOU have your own vision and when you focus on this you can see more clearly.

Imagine for yourself how you feel about yourself and life when you can see your best self and dream big.

Can you...

- imagine your best self and take the time to nurture this image?
- have insight into patterns and things that keep repeating?
- see things in a unique way and inspire someone else with your own vision?
- see life and learning as a gift?

If some of these things are not possible to feel you can see how easy it would be to close down from imagining, have trouble learning, feel you can follow those dreams or to get confused and lack focus on what matters to you.

But when these needs are met your imagination is great, you feel focused and ready to open to learning and like to see things differently.

When you open to your inner wisdom you will see just how magical you are. Believing that there is magic in you and all around you is the beginning of your own wisdom.

Focusing on your dreams you cultivate your inner wisdom like a craft. You may keep a record or a journal of your dreams – if not you might like to start.

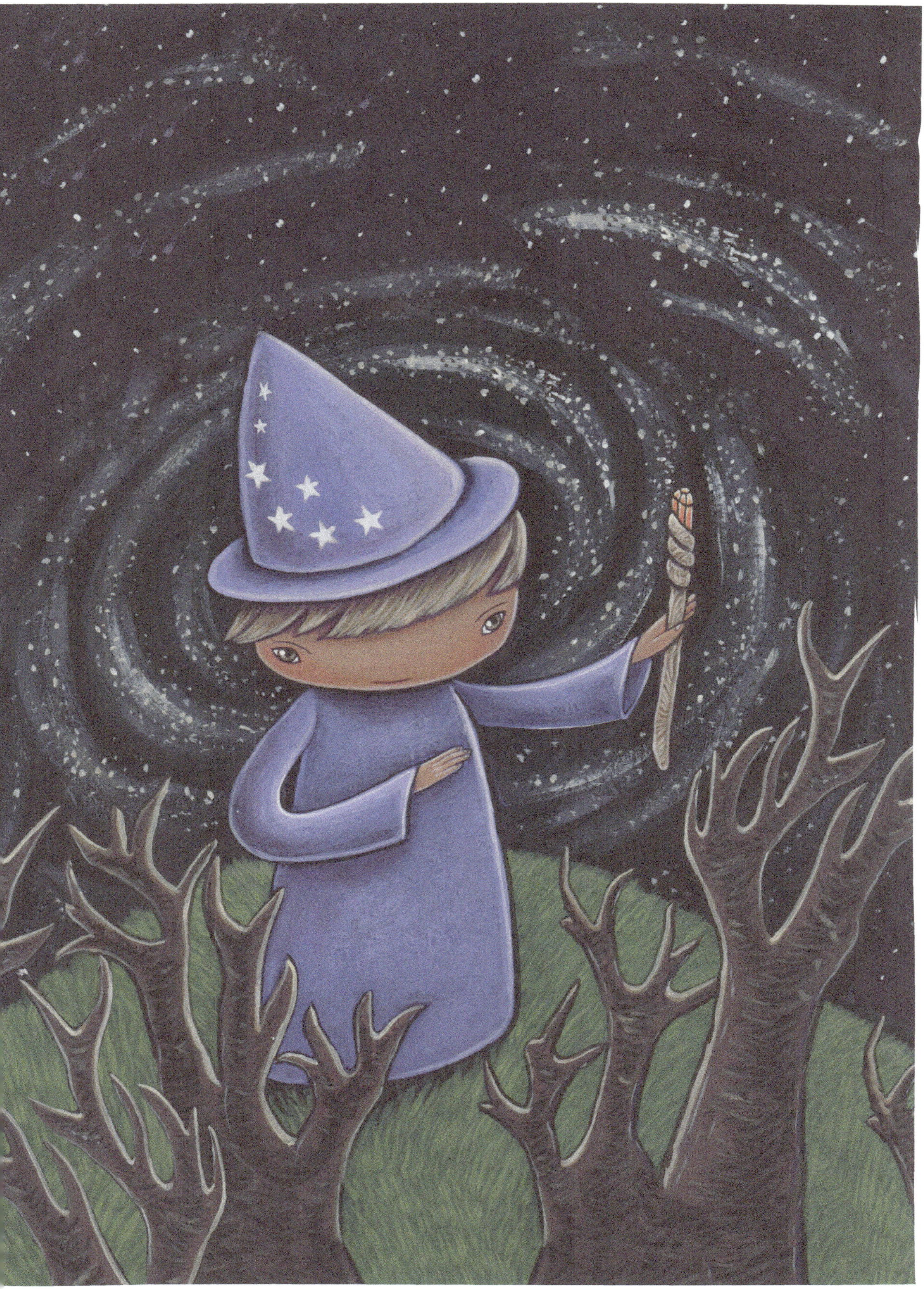

I see my way out of a learning challenge when....

I have plenty of time to figure something out.

I get to decide or choose what I imagine for me, not someone else.

I have time to play make believe in my own way.

I can get help and reassurance.

If someone paints a picture — or tells a story that I can see in my mind.

When I know my brain is working okay.

I can focus and there is not much noise or distraction.

When we have done a class meditation.

I am allowed to daydream about how things might turn out.

Circle the ones that feel most true to you, you may find that you have a few.

write the things that help you see more clearly in and around the image

Expansive feelings

focused   clear sight   insight

imagination   intuition

clarity   peaceful   intentions

concentration   accountability

open-minded   innovation

I feel clear when… ....
....

I feel focused when… ....
....

I feel determined when… ....
....

Contracting feelings

shy close-minded distracted
procrastinating lonely
judgement bad dreams
upset
unsettled sleep defeated
over-thinking
criticism confused
racing thoughts

I feel criticism when... ....
....

I feel distracted when... ....
....

I feel upset with my learning when... ....
....

Listen to your body's wisdom

There will be time when you don't always feel you can see your best self so it is important to trust your body and listen to what your body is telling you.

To listen to the body, remember we SENSE with our whole body.

Your Need to see is felt in the body locations of your brain, eyes, ears, nose, pineal gland, pituitary gland and nervous system.

See these highlighted on the next page.

- sinus
- eye
- ear
- brain
- pineal gland
- pituitary gland
- nose
- nervous system

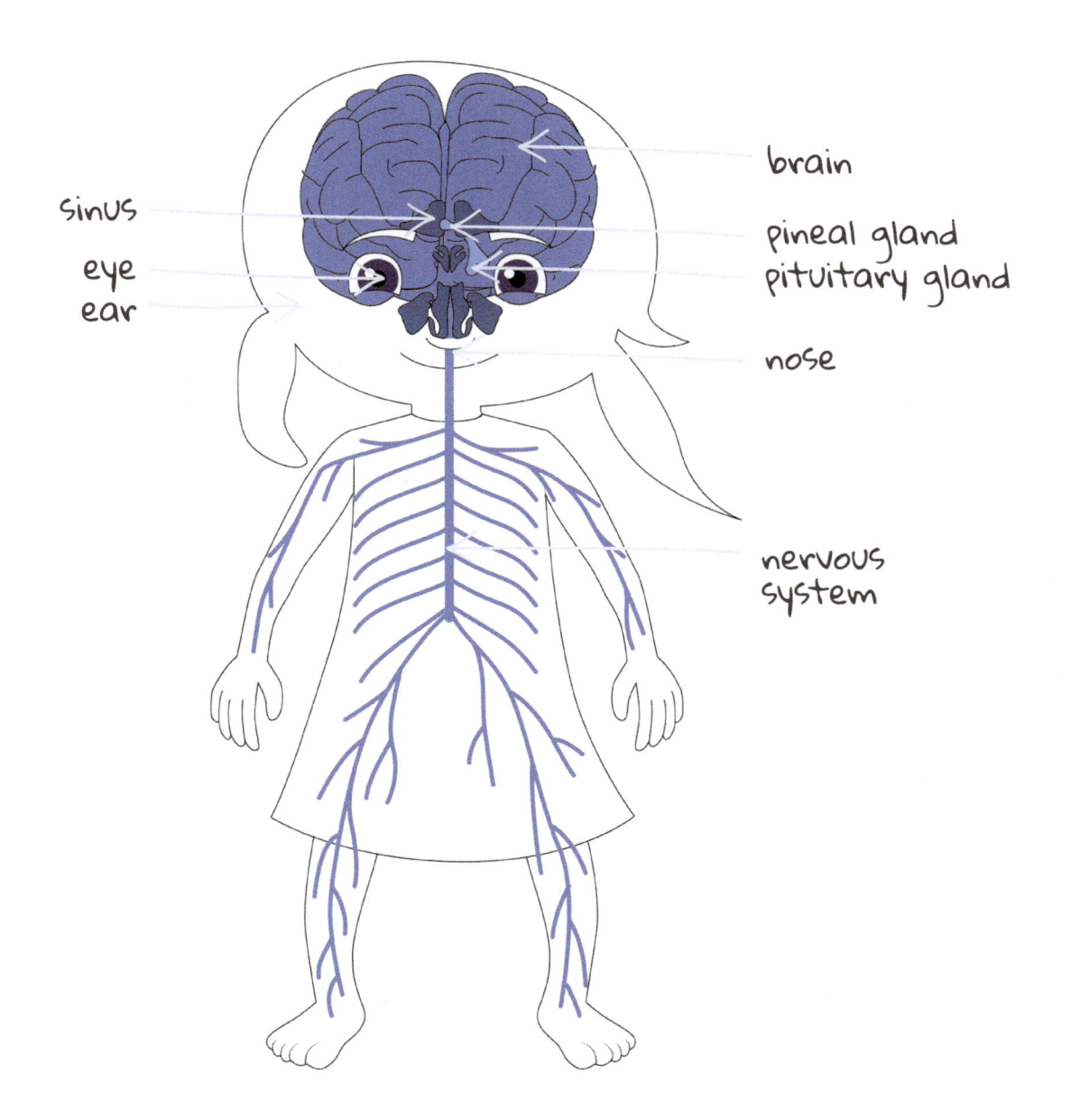

Body Mapping Your Feelings

BRAIN

Feel into your brain. Is it foggy or heavy? Is it clear and light? Is it jumpy? Is it quiet? Is it racing and swirling?

If so, I wonder what this might mean?

Sometimes you might feel you can't learn and that you'll never get it right and sometimes you learn easily and wonder why it has been so hard before.

Maybe none of these have meaning ...?

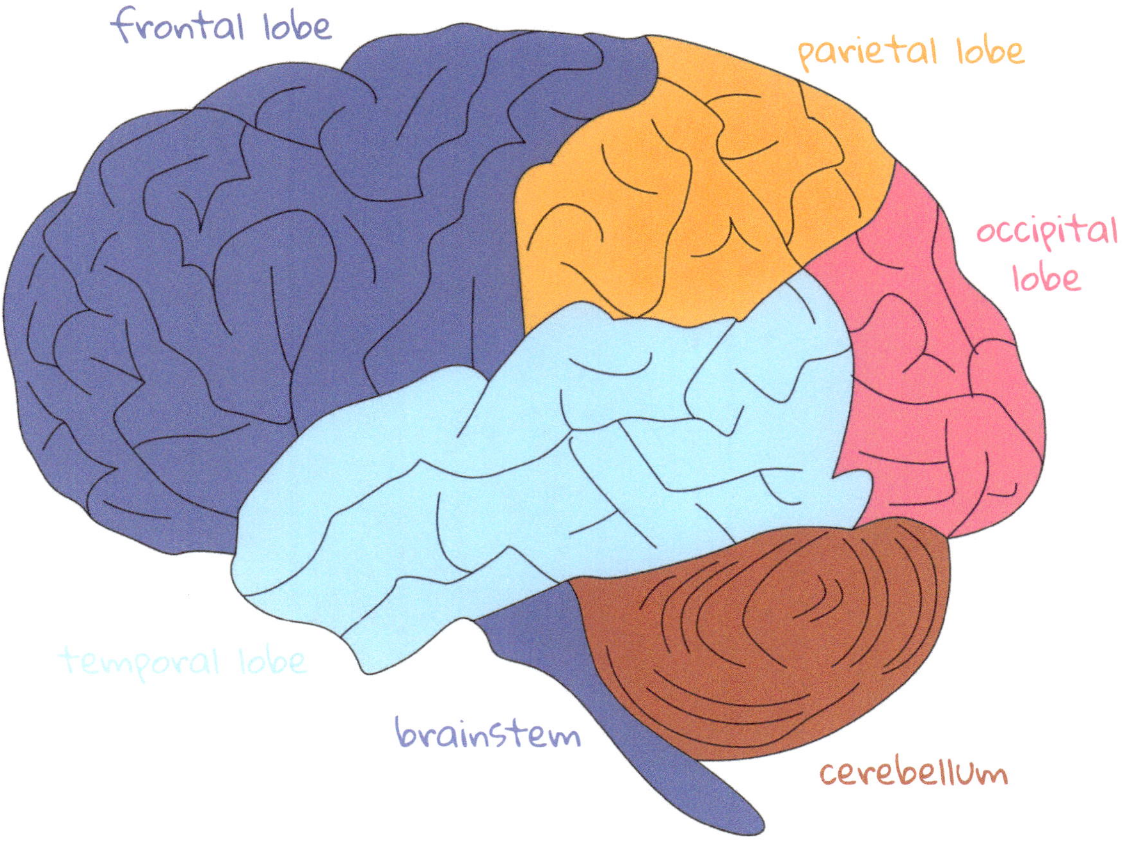
frontal lobe
parietal lobe
occipital lobe
temporal lobe
brainstem
cerebellum

Ask your brain to tell you what it needs?

Each part of the brain has a different function but each part has to work in harmony. Look at the image of the brain with different colours. Can you see the part of the brain called the brain stem? The brain stem connects to the nervous system and the nervous system's networks are connected to each of your 7 needs.

Send your attention and energy to your brain and imagine the energy going to all your needs.

SENSING INTO YOUR BRAIN

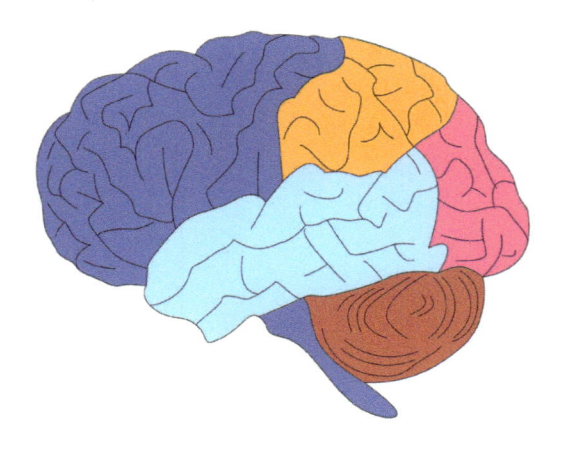

Write down what you feel on the blank page.

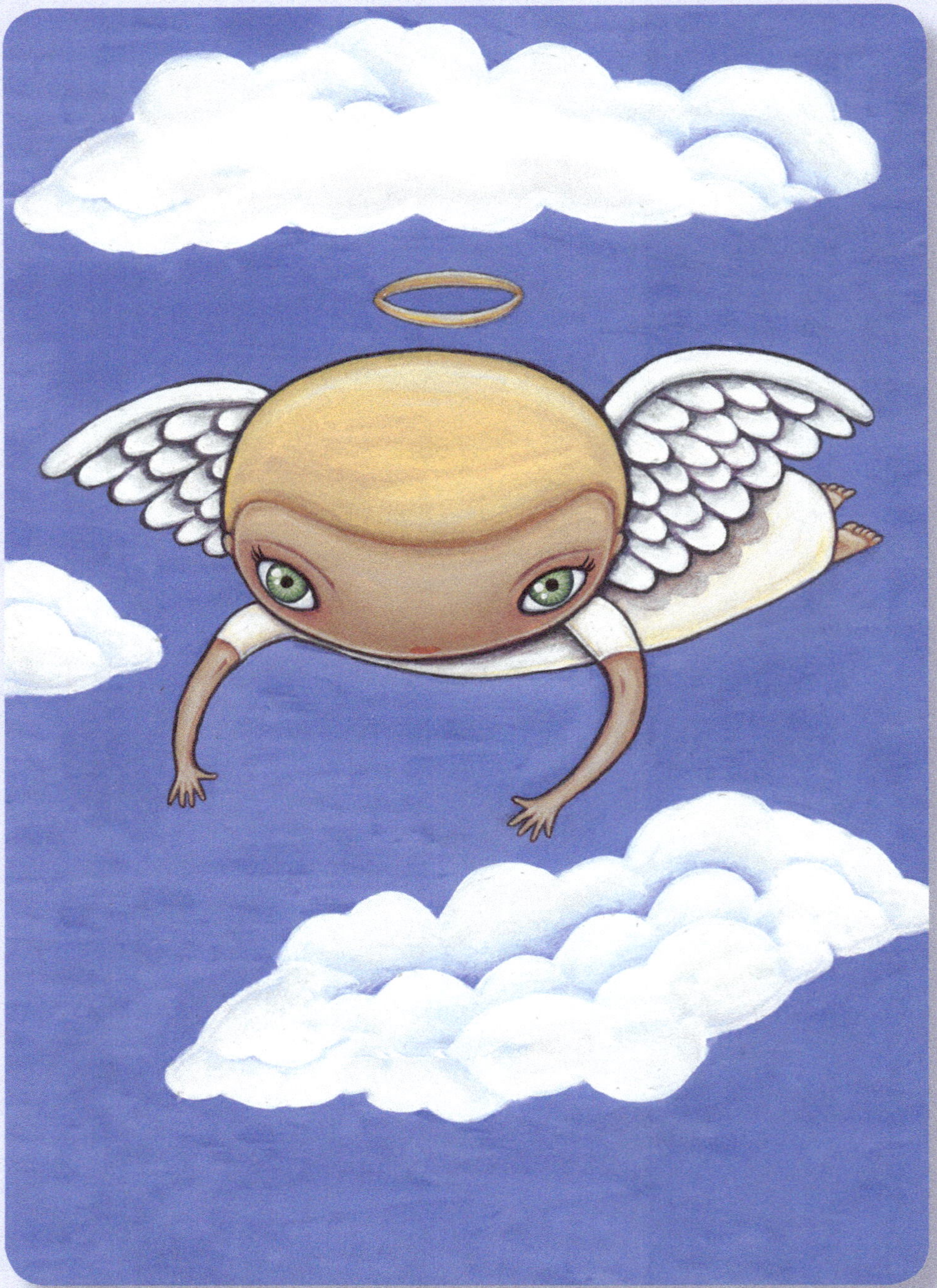

A Moment To Wonder

Do you believe in angels?
Can you see them?
Can you hear them?
Can you feel them?

Your visions and insights about things you cannot always see with your eyes, helps you to see things in another way. Take a moment NOW to pay attention to your imagination and draw or write about your visions.

You may like to meditate and take some quiet time to see what wonderful visions are waiting to be revealed to you.

Use your insights as a gift to guide yourself and others.

breathe

You can imagine a better vision and clarity anytime you want by connecting to your breath.

Breathe into the feelings of discomfort or unease in your body when you feel confused, distracted or not clear enough.

You don't need to have an answer as to why you are feeling what you are in this moment and you don't have to fix anything at all.

...just be in the wonder of YOU

FEEL all the FEELINGS that arise as prompts
THESE ARE IMPORTANT MESSAGES.
You can do this at anytime, anywhere you are ...
YOU SAY THE WORDS BELOW

breathing in...
I set my intention

breathing out...
I feel my mind open
to many possibilities

(Repeat these two sentences as
many times as you like)

Mind Mapping

A mind map is a way to get all your ideas out on paper. You write down all the words as they come to mind and all the ideas that you have.

SAY FOR INSTANCE YOU WANT TO MAKE A CREATION.

Think of all the things that come to mind and start writing and drawing them on the paper – this is a way to put all your amazing ideas and thoughts about the creation onto paper.

When you see the words written, it helps you to imagine even more things to write and draw.

Seeing things in front of you is – visual thinking and this tool helps you get clear and opens you to other possibilities in learning.

You will be better able to comprehend, recall and generate many new ideas if you give this a go.

Make your own mind map on the page opposite and don't hold back – let your imagination run wild!

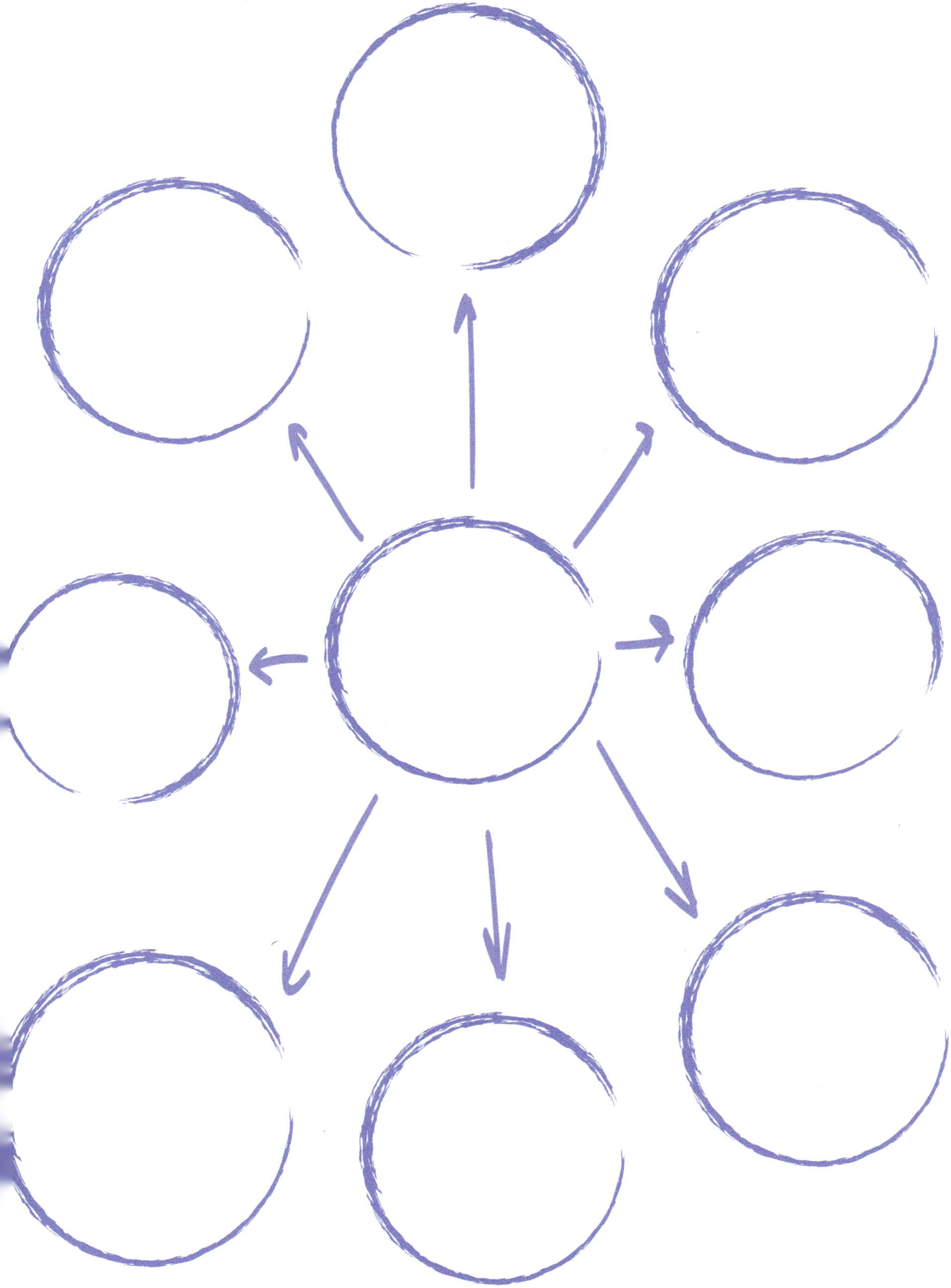

Map Your Family's WONDER

Interview time

Ask a family member – parents or grandparents what they to tell you about a time when they were worried about something that had not happened yet or something that might or might not happen in the future?

Record the answers.

What did they do?

What was their body telling them?

After you have done the interview you can think back to what you need to know when you are worried about something that has happened or something that is yet to happen ... and WONDER if this is something the grown-up you interviewed has felt too?

Wonder Jar

A Wonder Jar is a beautiful way to show you how your mind can sometimes appear 'shaken up'. You know that feeling when you are angry or sad and you feel like your thoughts are racing all over the place at a million miles per hour?

When you shake your Wonder Jar you can see this happening – glitter moving all over the place, swirling around and around and out of control.

But if you keep watching you will also see how slowly the glitter – or your thoughts and feelings – settle down. Slower and slower they move until they are perfectly still and settled again. Your mind works this way too and you can use your Wonder Jar to help you feel perfectly still and settled when you need to.

You will need

- A jar or bottle from the recycling bin – it can be plastic or glass
- 150 ml of clear Elmer's glue
- Glitter
- Small beads, stars, hearts or any other small items you wish to add
- Warm tap water
- Food colouring

To make

- Fill your jar or bottle about one third of the way full with the glue
- Add your glitter, sparkles and any other item you wish to add
- Fill the rest of the jar or bottle with the water
- Add a few drops of food colouring
- Put the lid or cap on and shake to see if you would like to add more glitter or colouring
- Once you have all the glitter you need in there, use either super-glue or a hot glue gun to seal the lid or cap onto the jar or bottle permanently. (You may need to ask a grown-up for help!)

Shake your Wonder Jar well and then watch it as it all slowly falls back into place. Keep watching it until every single last bit of glitter has fallen back into place.

WORD SEARCH

```
V I S I O N A R Y R U Y
D S L T S U C O F T M R
J W U K V K Q T Z U V R
B O R G A N I S E D M B
I M A G I N A T I O N C
D V A D B R S V Q W O B
P H O R H Q L B A H L Q
A K L E V B M I D O M Y
P N P A H C L A R I T Y
J F D M X H T F V A W H
B W O S G N I N R A E L
N N Y R O M E M O X Y K
```

ORGANISED   MEMORY
CLARITY   LEARNING
IMAGINATION   DREAMS
VISIONARY   FOCUS

My touchstone

When I am distracted

I feel ....

I need ....

This allows me to have clarity and feel I can see and imagine my best.

7.
I know

I am all Know-ing

The seventh of your Foundational Needs is your 'Need to Know'

Every child has the potential to know what they need.

YOU have so much self knowledge.

Do you have lots of questions about your self and the world that cannot be answered by anyone you know?

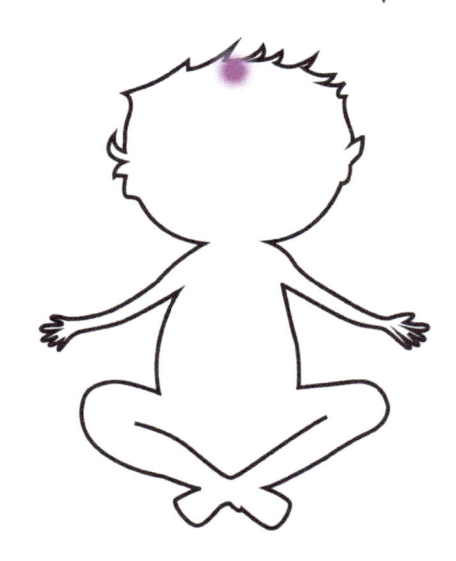

You might need to know about your purpose and what the meaning of your life is and why you do the things you do. You have such a wonder about you.

Every child needs to know their own brilliance and to have that knowing recognised.

Not everyone likes to hear what you know and some people will say you don't know much. This is not true, because I know that your body has so much knowledge and in a way you know more than you realise. It is like you know about a lot of things but you have not been able to get anyone to believe you.

Imagine for yourself how much you use your own self knowledge.

Can you...

- feel energies that others cannot?
- feel like you have a destiny that is important for you?
- feel connected to people, places and animals in a deeply moving way?

If other people do not know how to support or recognise that you have this self-knowledge you can see how easy it would be to be hypersensitive to the environment and people, frustrated, and feel a lack of connection or misunderstood.

But when these needs are met you feel very in tune with others, you have a feeling of a destined purpose to help the planet. Maybe, you will advocate for a cause so others benefit from your knowledge and help.

There will be times when you don't feel connected to your purpose or place in the universe. You might feel like you are from another planet. This is because you are a soul, who needs to feel, think and act in harmony. Trust your body and listen to what your body is telling you. You know so much more than what you can remember and you have a unique place in the universe.

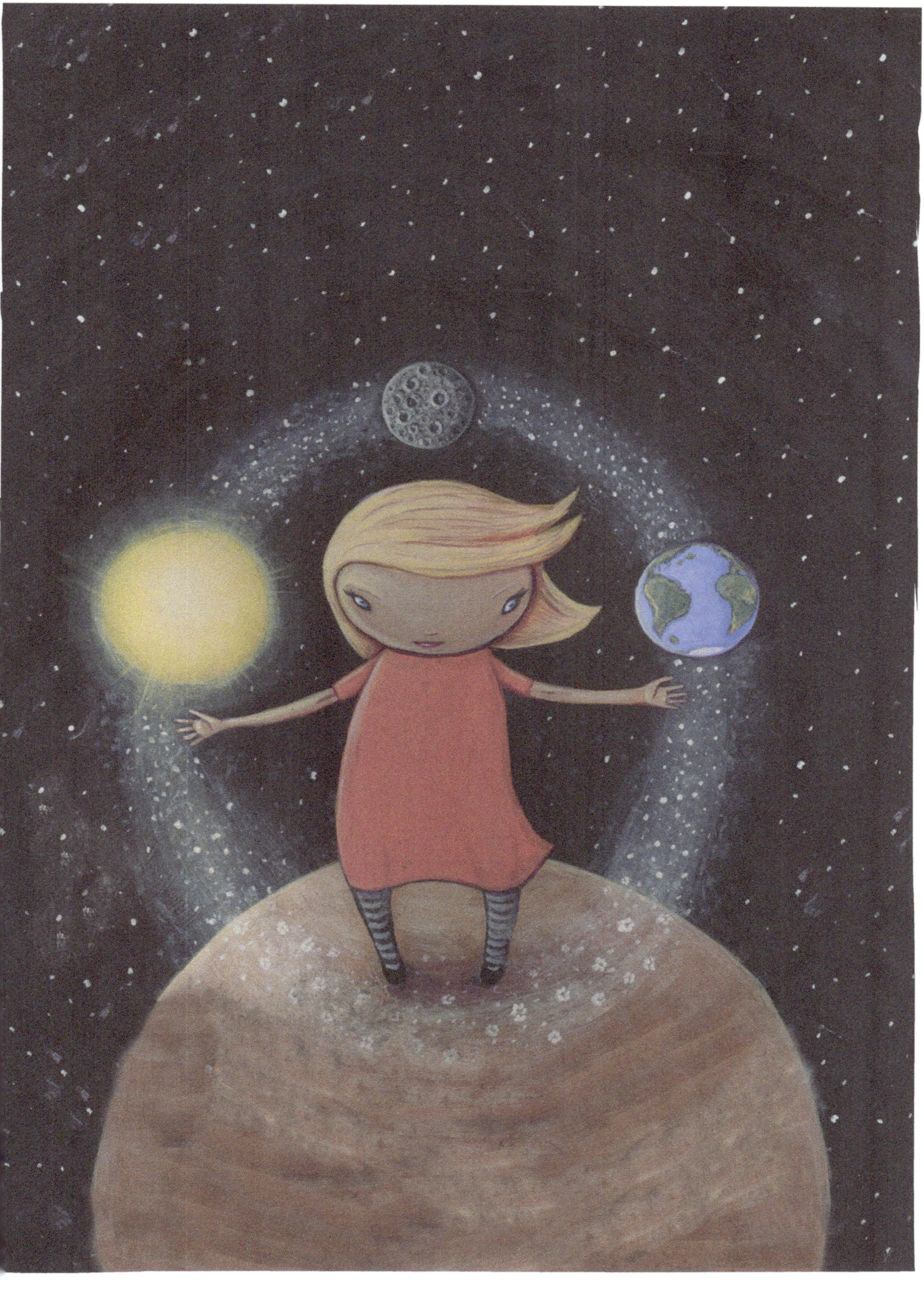

I feel connected to the universe when...

I am feeling joyful and share this joy with others.

I am taken seriously and valued.

I can question beliefs and thinking and can talk about things openly.

I can learn about other cultures.

I know the moon and sun affect how I feel.

I think about galaxies, space, stars and the universal energies.

I feel like I belong.

I have done meditation, asked for help and the help has come.

I am doing yoga or meditation and the energy is open and connected.

I am caring for the earth and planet.

People tell me it felt different without me there.

I feel like the things I value matter to others too.

Circle the ones that feel most true to you, you may find that you have a few.

write the things that you feel a unity with in and around the image

Unifying feelings

unity   Self-knowledge   purpose

divinity   at one   potential

home in god   meaning

connection

higher-power   wholeness

I feel connected when... ....
....

I feel whole when... ....
....

I feel purposeful when... ....
....

separating feelings

apathy   disdainful   self-doubt

dependent on others   attachment

addiction   fragmentation

unrealised potential

lack of meaning

lack of faith

Attached to Needing

I feel disconnected when… ……………………………………………………………
……………………………………………………………………………………………………

I feel full of self-doubt when… ………………………………………………………
……………………………………………………………………………………………………

I feel apathetic when… …………………………………………………………………
……………………………………………………………………………………………………

Listen to your body's wisdom

There will be times when you don't feel you know what you need and when this happens it is most important to trust your body and listen to what it is telling you.

Remember this type of listening is not like 'hearing with your ears' or 'thinking' with your brain — but by SENSING with your whole body.

Your Need to know is linked to the body locations of your skin, muscular system and skeletal system.

See these highlighted on the next page.

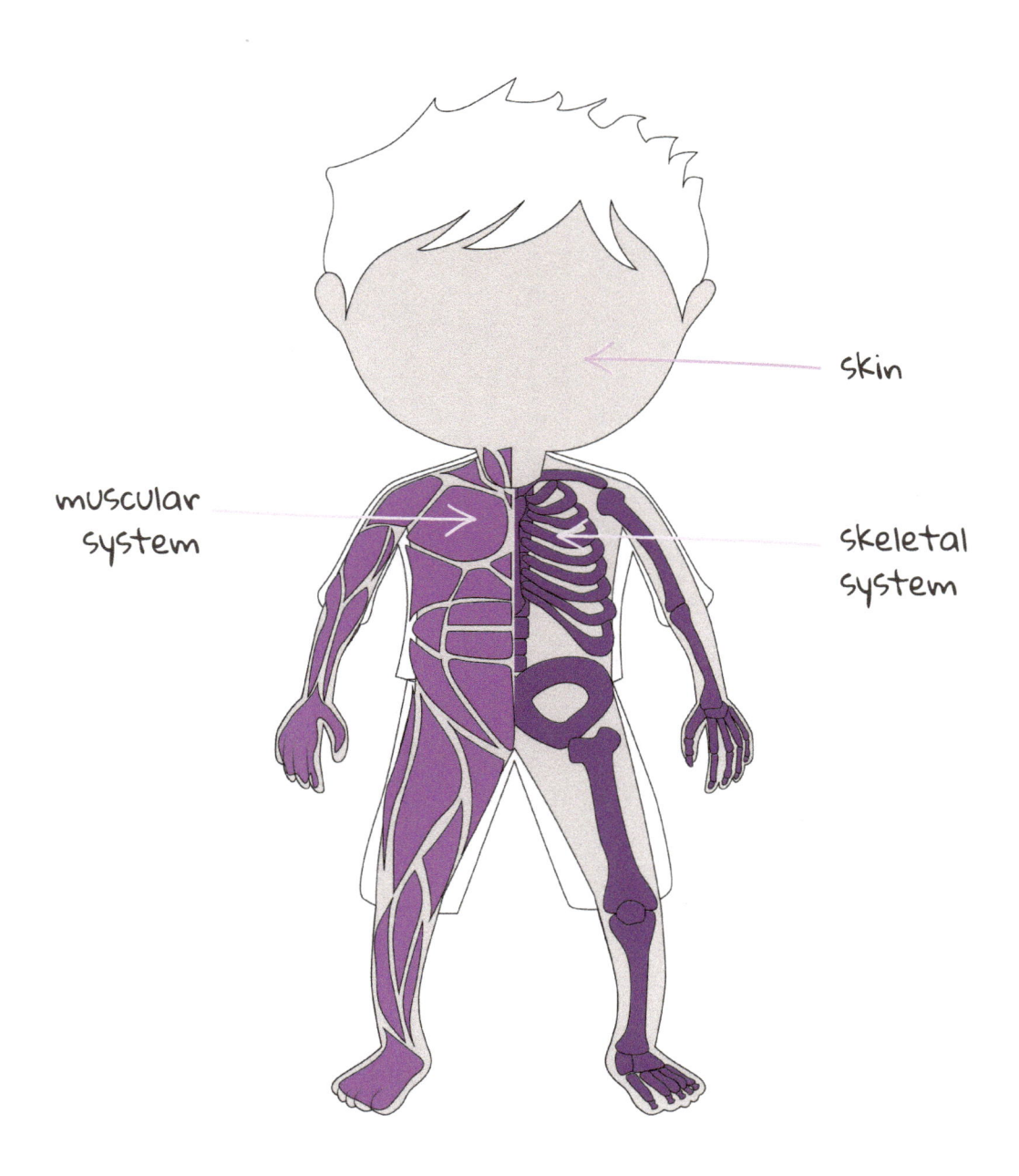

skin

muscular system

skeletal system

Body Mapping Your Feelings

SKIN

Feel into your skin. Is it soft or hard? Is it dry or moist? Is it light or is it dark? Is your skin healthy or is it a little tired?

I wonder what your skin means for you?

You might feel very comfortable in your skin and you don't even notice it at all. After all it has been growing with you since you were an embryo.

Your skin is like an antenna and picks up vital information from the environment. It is like a protective coat. Your skin is the largest organ in your body.

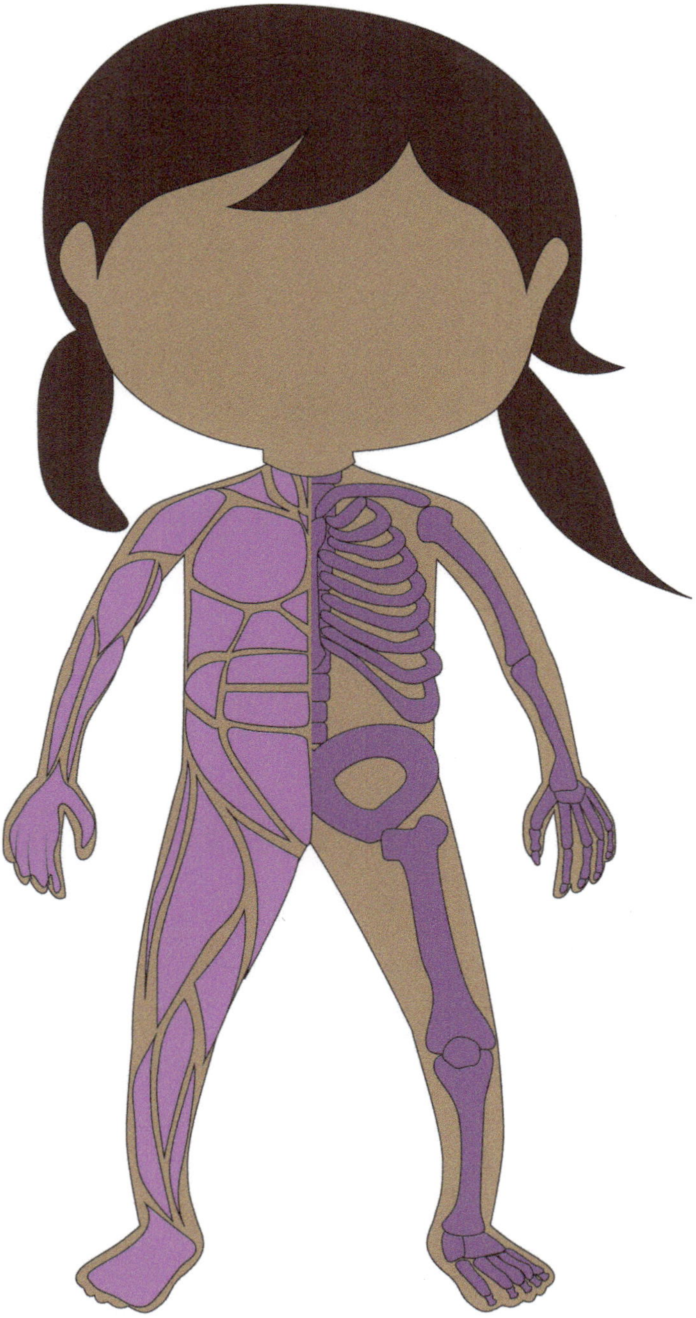

Ask your skin to tell you what it needs?

Do you love the skin you're in?

Do you feel protected by your skin?

SENSING INTO YOUR SKIN

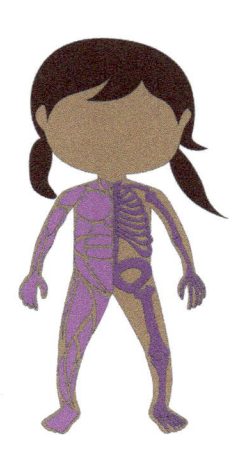

Write down what you feel on the next page.

You can also feel into your skeletal system and muscular system and how much these parts of you support your Need to Know – look to the map of body parts on page 221. You might also sense into these parts and write down how these parts of your body might feel for you.

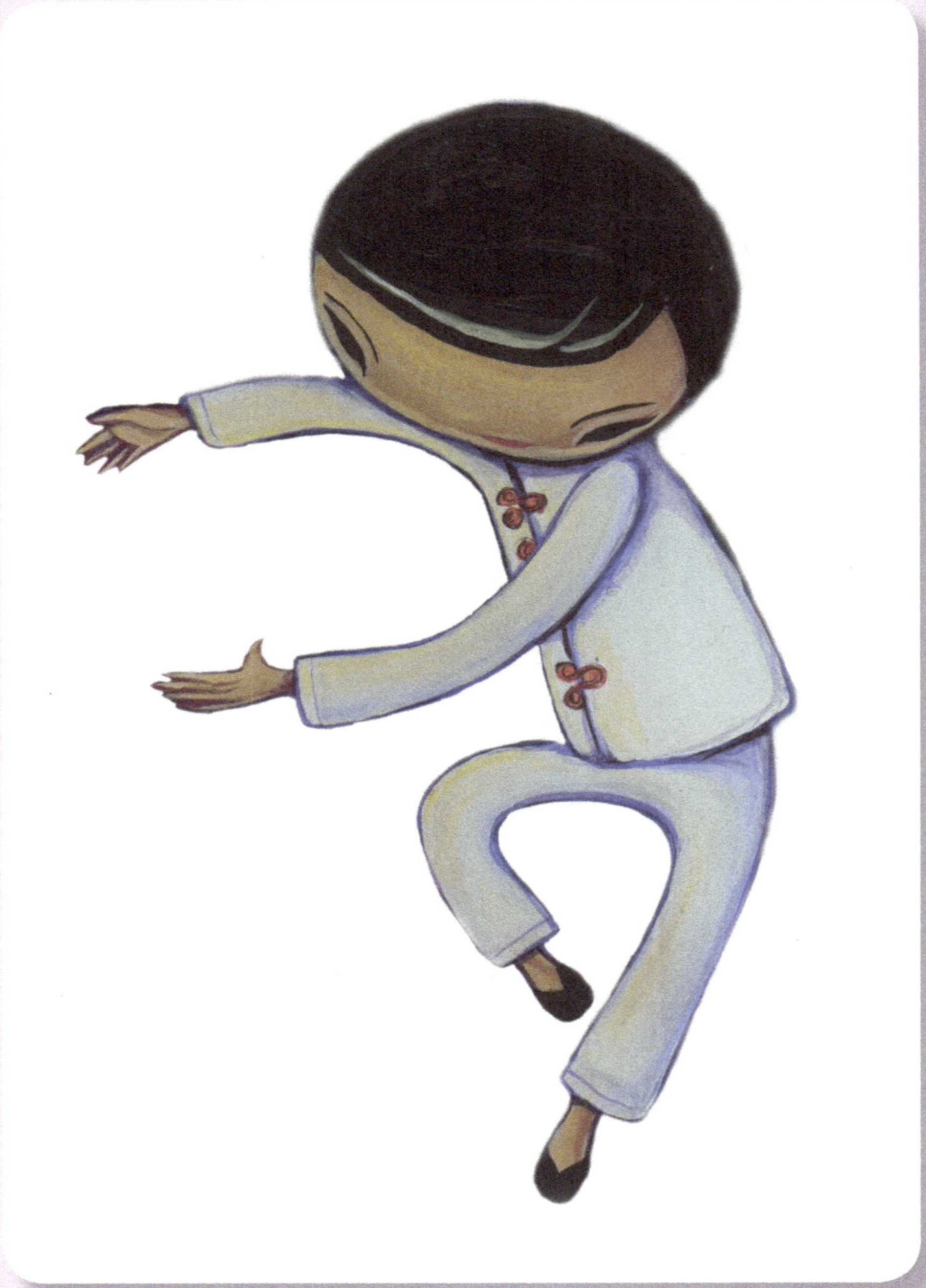

A Moment To Wonder

If you doubt your self-awareness or your divine nature, you can take a moment to feel into your unique brilliance.

Your brilliance is not just important for you, but the whole of the world. You are a part of the whole and anything that you do effects everything and everyone else.

If you feel at home in your body it means that you feel at home in the world.

The world would not be the same without your brilliance and you have a special soul destiny to activate which is your place in the world.

What makes you feel at home in your body?

How do you get that feeling of home
— when you are not at home?

breathe

You can imagine you always know what you need by connecting to your breath.

Breathe into the feelings of discomfort or unease in your body when you feel irritated, trapped, lonely or lost.

You don't need to have an answer as to why you are feeling what you are in this moment and you don't have to fix anything at all.

...just be in the wonder of YOU

FEEL all the FEELINGS that arise as prompts
THESE ARE IMPORTANT MESSAGES.
You can do this at anytime, anywhere you are ...
YOU SAY THE WORDS BELOW

breathing in...
I ask for the information I need to come to me

breathing out...
I have faith that all will be okay

(Repeat these two sentences as many times as you like)

Map Your Family's WONDER

Interview time

Ask a family member – parents or grandparents to tell you about a time when they had faith in something even though life was uncertain. How did they trust that all would be okay?

Record the answers.

What did they do?

What was their body telling them?

After you have done the interview you can think back to what you need to know ... and WONDER if this is something the grown-up you interviewed has felt too?

Crystal Grid

Did you know that children have a special power to connect with the universe? Grown-ups lose this special power because they tend to think more about boring grown-up things! But YOU are so in tune with the universal energy and with feeling connected to the past, present and future – and your 'wholeness'.

The universe is teaching you lessons to help you every day and, in every moment, you are absorbing information in the form of energy.

Playing with crystals or creating a crystal grid helps you tap into this universal energy as well as far-away galaxies, distant planets and any other information that is out there.

Instructions

Use your intuition and choose a few crystals. Because children are so in tune with their universal energy, you will naturally pick a crystal that you are drawn to and has meaning for you.

You can either pick a few and make a crystal grid, place a few crystals on your bedside table to help you sleep or carry one in your pocket to school to help with anxiety issues.

Crystals are amazing – each type has different healing properties to help you feel whole and balanced.

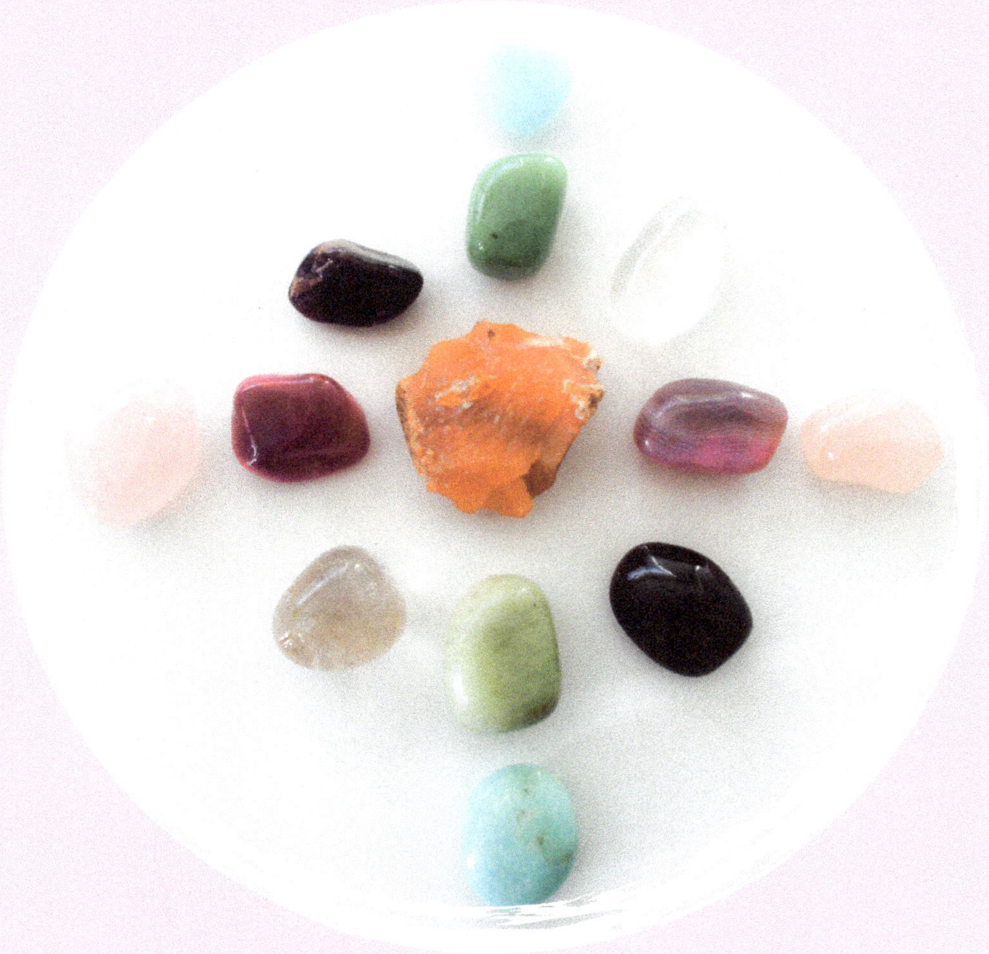

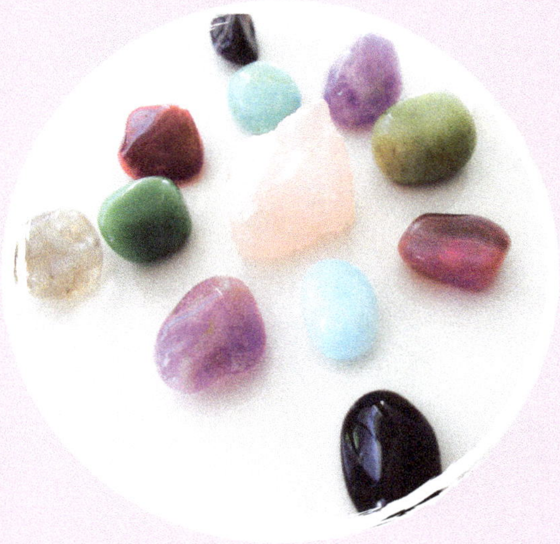

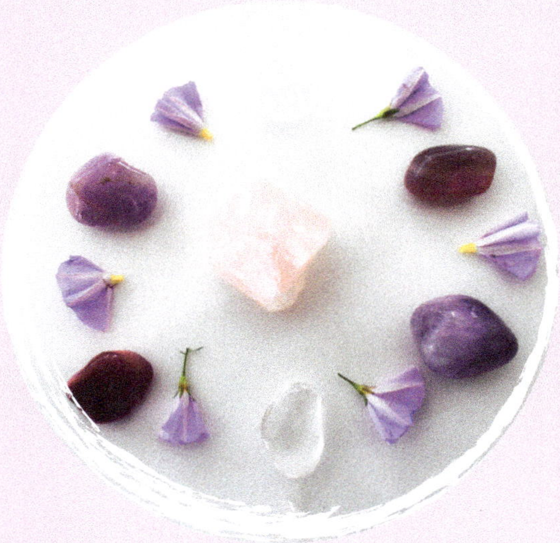

WORD SEARCH

```
V P Y F W V K C A V T A
X O S K A O Q O W N O B
M T R B I R F N D H O W
E E B N U W L N Z S G H
A N K T C D T E Z W D O
N T Y T I N U C A K U L
I I X Y J Y P T L G H E
N A R K O F L I B A I N
G L Z B U J U O X N N W
B E L I E F K N R X V M
U T V S J P U R P O S E
G Z Y T I N I V I D Q Y
```

UNITY
PURPOSE
POTENTIAL
CONNECTION

BELIEF
WHOLE
MEANING
DIVINITY

My touchstone

When I am lonely

I feel ....

I need ....

This makes me know I am connected and whole.

Look at

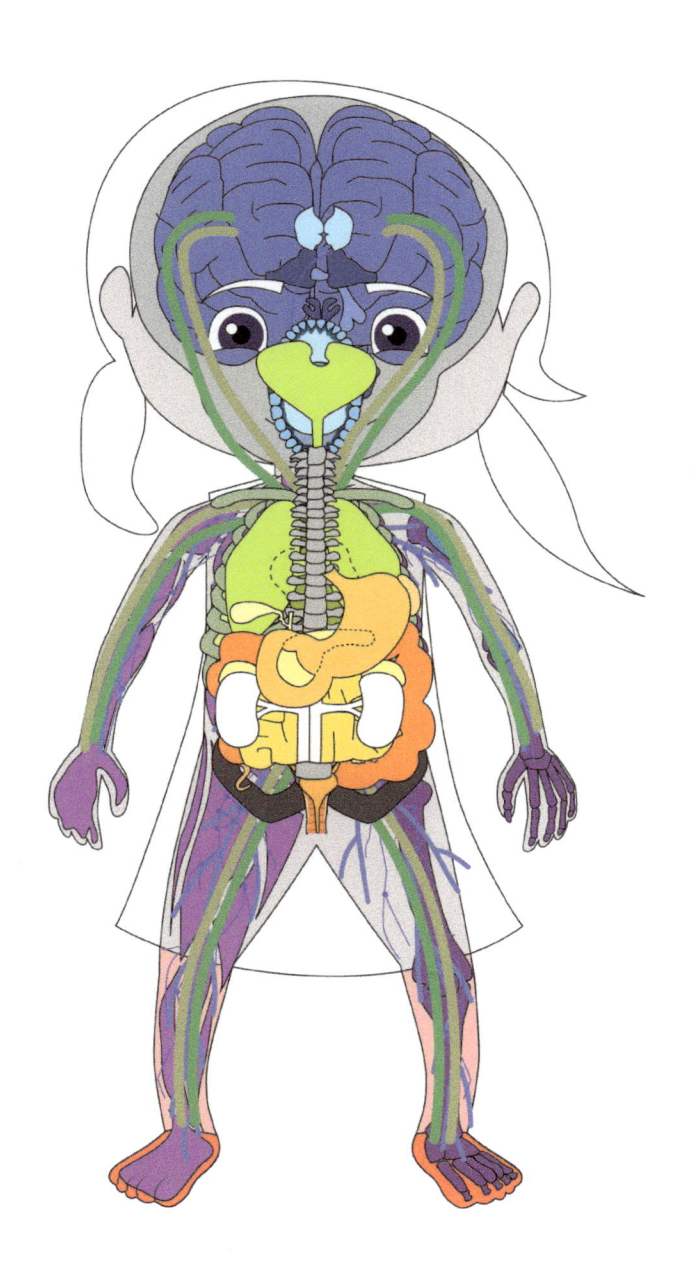

THE WONDER OF YOU

As you have immersed yourself in each of your 7 needs, YOU have absorbed so much information. You have come to see and feel the WONDER that lives inside every cell of your body.

By learning a new way of listening through SENSING with your whole body you have felt things that you might not have felt before.

You have learnt how the things you feel and think really do have an affect on how you behave. And if you have a behaviour that does not feel good for you — you can sense into what the meaning of the behaviour is and look to the unmet need it is trying to communicate.

The wonderful thing about this journal is that it really is not about how any one else feels but you. Of course everyone shares the 7 common needs but what we feel in our bodies is unique and will be different for everyone. That is why the things that we feel and think don't always have the same meaning for everyone.

You are the one who decides the meaning for YOU!

Listen to your body's wisdom

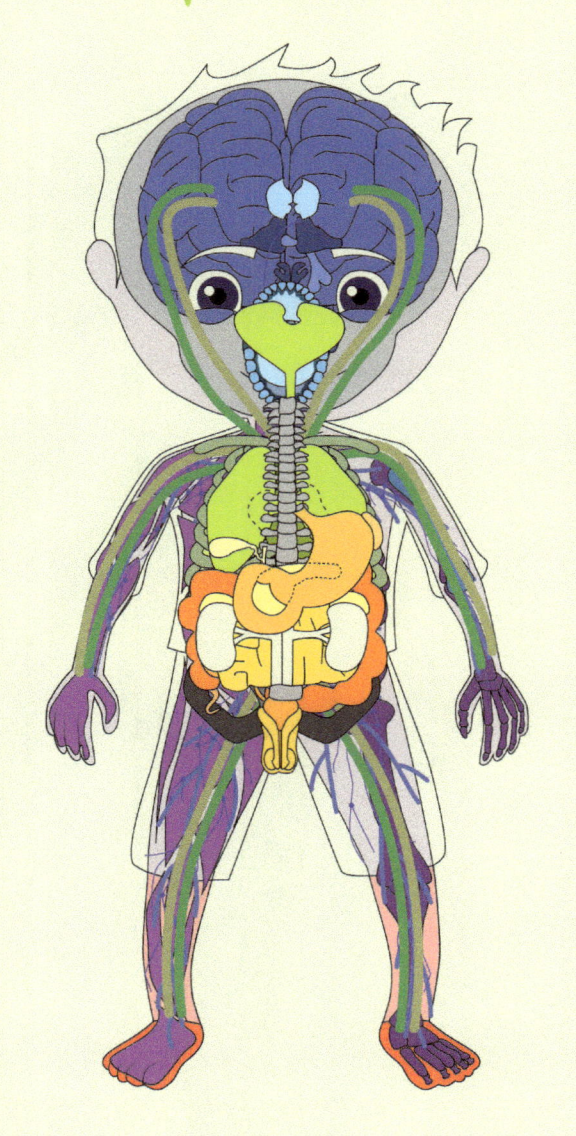

YOU can continually discover messages about
The WONDER OF YOU. Even when things look overwhelming
and feel big, if you find the unmet need beneath the
challenge, and SENSE with your whole body, you can
interpret the meaning of your challenge.

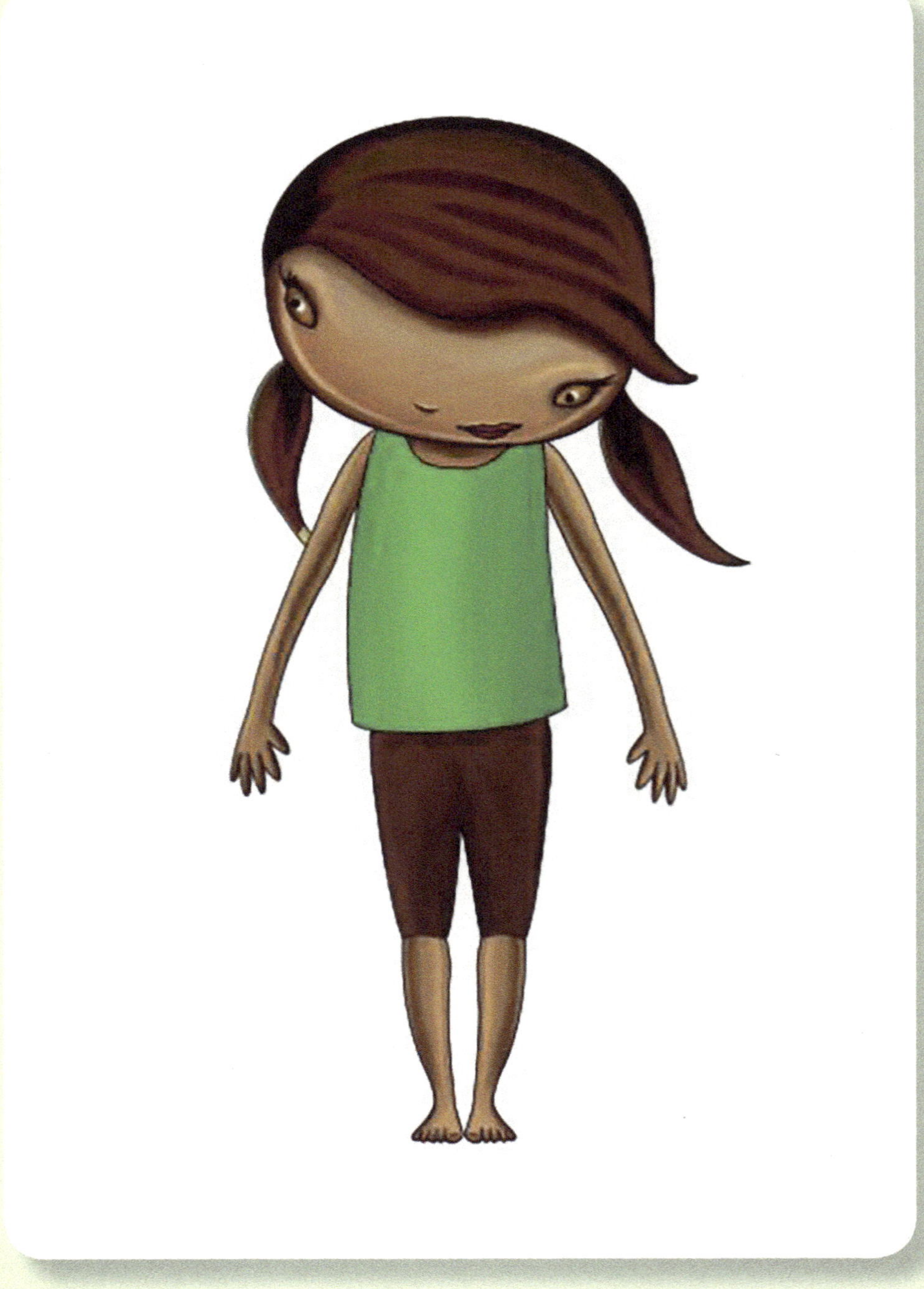

A Moment To Wonder

Now you have practiced being in the WONDER of You, you can pause for a moment anytime and let go of your concerns and worries knowing that all your needs are taken care of and that your needs matter.

Whenever you are standing and breathing you can take a moment to position yourself.

YOU SAY THE WORDS BELOW

breathing in...
I open to the wonder of me

breathing out...
I acknowledge the wonder in you

Map Your Family's WONDER

By being in the wonder with your family by asking your parent, grandparents, uncles and aunts as well a brother or sister how they feel and what they need — YOU now have an image of your common challenges. You also now know that we all share the same feelings and needs.

You will most likely find that there is a pattern — that something like this has been present for someone close to you. This truly is how connected we all are.

So remember when you are really stuck you can ask yourself ...

I wonder if anyone in my family has ever felt this way or had this thing happen?

Who knows what hidden treasure you will discover when you remain in the Wonder!

Revisit the answers you wrote down in each section and continue to add things to the list of common patterns that appear in you that come from your family and ancestors.

You might like to imagine them bowing in gratitude to you for passing on the wonder to all the future generations too.

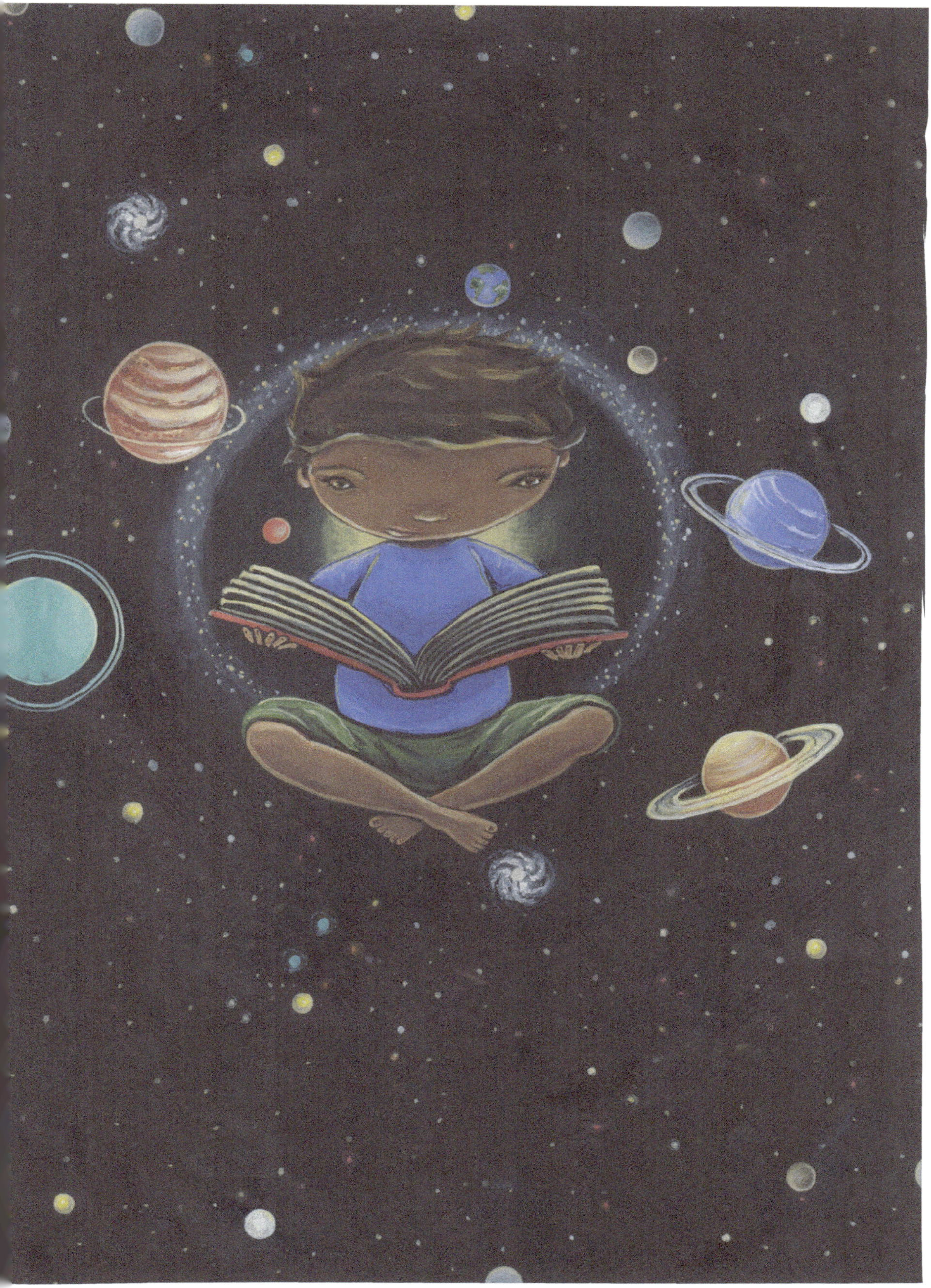

I may feel….	I NEED	Look to my body for clues – Anatomy
unsafe, afraid of change, a fear when separated from mum or dad.	**I AM SAFE** The Need to be Safe and Secure	Legs, bones, feet, rectum, immune system
stuck, impulsive, no emotional control, fussy, uncertain or obsessive	**I AM FREE** The Need to Feel	Reproductive system, urinary system, bladder, endocrine
ready to give up powerless, shame, withdrawn, indecisive, over active	**I ACT** The Need to Act	Stomach and digestive system, adrenal glands
angry, unloved, sadness, sorrow, hurt, irritable	**I LOVE** The Need to Love	Heart, circulation, respiration (asthma) breathing
Unnoticed, nervous Uncertain of expression yelling – silence	**I SPEAK** The Need to Speak	Throat, mouth, voice (speech issues), teeth and gums, lymphatic system
distracted, confused shy, lack of focus, Unsettled sleep or dreams	**I IMAGINE** The Need to See	Brain (Learning challenges – Focus) Eyes, ears, nose (sinus) Nervous system
frustrated, hypersensitive to the environment and people. lack of connection	**I KNOW** The Need to Know	SKIN (issues) Muscular (Growing pains) Skeletal (bones, posture and stance)

Things I can do	I can Affirm
BREATHE EXERCISE. Learn about what your body is saying. Ground to the earth through being in nature and meditation.	It is safe for me to be here I trust my bodies wisdom
BREATHE EXERCISE It is normal for you to experience a wide range of emotions. Accept all of your feelings.	I accept my feelings I move easily and effortlessly
BREATHE EXERCISE Follow your own intuition. Feel into what you should do? Try to follow your own lead sometimes.	I honour the power within me I am enough
BREATHE EXERCISE Have quality time with a loved one. Spend time in devotion and loving service.	I am worthy of love I am loved and loving
BREATHE EXERCISE Use positive vibration words.	I can express myself I am heard
BREATHE EXERCISE Imagine yourself as your greatest self. Set daily or weekly intentions.	I see all things in clarity I can manifest my vision
BREATHE EXERCISE You can aim for a higher purpose in any situation.	Divinity resides within me: I know my unique brilliance

Acknowledgements

What a joy it has been to create this journal. I have so much gratitude for its creation.

My sons Dillon and Austin – thank you for igniting a new curiosity in me when I became your mother. As I watched the wonder of you both unfold I also realigned with my souls purpose. I made this from what I learnt from you.

To my mum and dad, thank you for imparting such wisdom and persistence on to me and to all my siblings and their children and grandchildren for the joy of family life you bring me.

Melissa Watkins, for your holding space for the process of creating this wonder and your dedication to Childosophy and me. Thank you for helping my dream become a reality. Thank you Sophie Mitchell for all the run around, I appreciate you. Thank you Jasmine Watkins for your help with the activities and bringing your little heart and hands to this journal.

Melanie Bedford, thank you for your art, I am so grateful for the growth from the original work. Jodie Beckley, for reworking the art and for your design elements. Michelle Pirovich @ thesqueezebox for your work putting it all together and creating such a beautiful journal.

My Childosophy practitioners, and all my clients past, present and future, the wonder of you is my continued inspiration.

Dr Maxine Thérèse is a leading expert in Children's Wellbeing and the founder of Childosophy — a complete philosophy and affirmative approach to children's needs. Maxine's professional, academic and personal life has been guided by a push to find better ways to assist the development of children. Maxine speaks at various events, conducts practitioner, teacher and parenting seminars and consults with children and adults in clinical practice. Maxine is proudly the mother of two adult sons.

www.childosophy.com

Lightning Source UK Ltd.
Milton Keynes UK
UKHW052357200519
342996UK00004B/14/P

9 780994 641373